LOUGH DERG

LOUGH DERG

ST. PATRICK'S PURGATORY

BY

ALICE CURTAYNE

LONDON AND DUBLIN
BURNS OATES & WASHBOURNE, LTD.
1944

First Published 1944

NIHIL OBSTAT:
GEORGIUS CAN. SMITH, S.Th.D., Ph.D.,
Censor Deputatus.

IMPRIMATUR:
E. MORROGH BERNARD,
Vic. Gen.

WESTMONASTERII, *die* 16 *Junii,* 1944.

MADE AND PRINTED IN ÉIRE
BY SEALY, BRYERS & WALKER
FOR
BURNS OATES & WASHBOURNE LTD.

ACKNOWLEDGMENT

GRATEFUL thanks are due to the Most Reverend Eugene O'Callaghan, D.D., Bishop of Clogher, for having written the Introduction and for his kindly interest in this book ; to the Right Reverend Monsignor Patrick Keown, P.P., V.G., Carrickmacross, for the uncountable ways he helped me when writing it and for reading and correcting the manuscript ; to Sir Shane Leslie and to his publishers, Messrs. Burns, Oates & Washbourne, Ltd., for permission to quote freely from *St. Patrick's Purgatory, Lough Derg*, 1932 ; to the Franciscan Fathers, Merchants' Quay, Dublin, who so kindly gave me facilities to copy H. of Saltrey's narrative from their great treasure, Colgan's *Trias Thaumaturga ;* to the Rev. E. C. Ward, Prior of Lough Derg, for his advice and help with Chapter V ; to the Rev. John F. Murphy, P.P., Aghabog, and to my nephew, Rev. P. Lynn, A.M., both of whom provided and checked translations of H. of Saltrey's narrative and other extracts ; to the Very Rev. Denis Canon McGrath, Parochial House, Bundoran, for supplying some interesting details of the Franciscan tenure of Lough Derg ; to Mrs. Nessa Doran, who carried out all the necessary research work in Irish ; to Mrs. A. M. Osler, who did the research work in the British Museum Library, London, and procured photostat copies of bibliographies and maps ; and to Mr. Pat Monaghan, caretaker of the sanctuary, who so many times and with such commendable patience, rowed me around the lake in the off-season.

DEDICATION

To the Right Reverend Monsignor Patrick
Keown, P.P., V.G., this book is dedicated
with gratitude and affection

CONTENTS

CHAPTER   PAGE

Foreword VIII

I. The Coming of St. Patrick I

II. Lough and Islands 14

III. Mediaeval Fame 27

IV. Caves and Fantasies 41

V. The Irish Way 56

VI. Suppression 70

VII. The Penal Night 88

VIII. The Nineteenth Century 108

IX. Resurgence 138

X. The Basilica 152

XI. Making the Pilgrimage 167

XII. Spirit of the Pilgrimage 179

Notes and Documentation 185

Bibliography 188

Index 191

FOREWORD

THE rapid growth in recent years of the Pilgrimage of Lough Derg, due largely to the fostering care of successive Popes who bestowed upon the Pilgrimage so many singular marks of the Church's approval, has drawn public attention to the venerable shrine, and created a desire for definite information regarding its origin and development. Many books have been written on St. Patrick's Purgatory, viewed from different aspects, but there was still room for a consecutive record of the Pilgrimage from its foundation by our National Apostle fifteen hundred years ago down to the present day.

Dean O'Connor's learned work on Lough Derg brings us down to 1881. From an historic point of view, the last sixty years have been perhaps the most eventful in the life of the Pilgrimage. During that period the independence of Station Island was secured; the ferry rights have been established; suitable buildings were erected for the accommodation of the pilgrims; the noble Basilica, which stands as the realization of the hopes of generations, and the embodiment of the faith, hope and generosity of the people of Ireland, has been completed.

With the destruction of the buildings in Lough Derg and the expulsion of the Franciscans in 1632, all the records of its glorious past were also destroyed. The result is that the historian has to rely for many important facts on the living voice of tradition. Tradition, when jealously guarded and carefully handed down is a reliable source of information.

Lough Derg being an integral part of the Irish Church was, like the Church, submitted to all the calumnies and persecutions that could be devised by the enemies of our holy Faith: but like the Church it has emerged triumphantly from the prolonged night of sorrow and suffering, and we find it to-day more vigorous, more promising, more popularly known than it was at any time of its history. It is an eloquent tribute to the Irish people that the penitential exercises, severe as they are, have been handed down without any substantial modification from the earliest time to our own day.

It is fortunate in the interest of Lough Derg that the task of compiling and giving to the public a complete history of St. Patrick's Purgatory, Lough Derg, has been undertaken by the gifted writer, Mrs. Rynne, who as Alice Curtayne, the distinguished author and journalist, is familiarly known in every Catholic home in Ireland.

Mrs. Rynne with her characteristic thoroughness and conscientious adherence to truth, has spared neither time nor labour, nor has she left any avenue unexplored, in her endeavour to acquire accurate information. The result is a most absorbing book breathing a spirit of warm affection and enthusiasm for that ancient shrine.

I wish to endorse the tribute of this book to Right Rev. Monsignor Keown for his work in fostering the development of the Pilgrimage.

To those readers who have been to Lough Derg, it will be a joy to find their spiritual experiences and reactions so ably expressed ; to all its readers it will be an urge to make the pilgrimage and become sharers in so ancient and so glorious a tradition.

It gives me great pleasure to approve of the publication of this book, and to recommend it to the public.

✠ EUGENE O'CALLAGHAN.

Bishop's House,
   Monaghan.
     2nd June, 1944.

LOUGH DERG

I. THE COMING OF ST. PATRICK

THERE is a lake called Lough Derg in County Donegal which has acquired extraordinary fame both in Christian history and in general literature. Natural beauty, however, does not account for that renown, as austerity is the character of the scene. Situated in the south-eastern tip of the county, this expanse of water is not even enhanced by nearness to the celebrated coast-line. The lake is extensive, six miles by four miles in area, and surrounded by low, heather-clad mountains, mostly unrelieved by either trees or cultivation, unremarkable in contour, forming a landscape that is usually a monotonous monochrome of either brown or grey tints. There is nothing to allure the eye here and no scenery in the accepted sense.

It is one of the loneliest places on earth. Its boulder-strewn shores, thirteen miles in circumference, seem to have retained all their original wildness. On some of the southern hill-slopes in recent years, the afforestation authorities have planted several thousand larch, spruce and fir-trees, whose green spires are now showing above the nursing knee-high heather. But there is little other cultivation to be seen. Only one main road leads to the lake, that from the small town of Pettigo, four miles distant. This road ends at the ferry, where there is a house and a few other buildings. No road, and not even a defined path, goes around the lake. There are the remains of some ruined homesteads on the southern shores ; but in all that rolling expanse of barren hill and moorland, in which this water is set, only a couple of houses are visible. These dwellings look like white dots in the hills ; they are far away from one another, and approached by paths invisible from any distance, so that they seem to emphasize the uninhabited character of this whole region.

It is remarkable how completely the exterior world is shut out. Those trackless hills enfold the lake as though to hide it. The nearest railway station is four miles away. Despite the ancient and enduring interest that invests this place, it has never attracted any permanent dwellers. The barren soil seems to forbid the formation of homesteads on it.

The lake surface is broken by numerous scattered islands, the greater number of which are just rocks without either historical or scenic interest. The fame of this region centres around only two of the larger islands : Station Island, more correctly called the Island of Saint Patrick's Purgatory, and Saints' Island, two miles northwest of it. But it is to Station Island that the eyes of all newcomers to the lake shore are immediately attracted, because of its many clustered buildings, dominated by a great church with a green dome. Very little of this island surface is visible from the shore, and the buildings give the impression of resting on the water. As a fact, every available yard of the Island has long ago been built over. Most of the church rests upon piles driven into the bed of the lake ; only its entrance porch is built upon the island.

Fifteen thousand people, on an average, come to Saint Patrick's Purgatory every year, remaining on Station Island for the greater part of three days in order to do penance there. The number, fifteen thousand, is impressive enough when it is explained that the Island is open to receive these pilgrims for only ten weeks each year : from June 1st to August 15th. Moreover, it is claimed that this curious, and indeed uninviting pilgrimage has now been observed for nearly fifteen hundred years almost without interruption. (During persecution spells, of course, there were occasional compulsory interruptions). This little lake island has thus been the centre of prayer and penance and has had no other purpose since Patrician days. During all that time, it has completely escaped commercialisation. There is hardly another devotional centre in the Christian world of which this can be said ; certainly there is no other such place in Ireland.

One of the very strongest traditions in the Irish Church is the belief that Saint Patrick himself originated the penance on Station Island. Like so many very cherished institutions, the documentary evidence for this is meagre, all Irish history being extremely badly documented. There are only two original sources from which we may seek for details of Saint Patrick's missionary work in Ireland : the *Tripartite Life* and the *Breviarium* of Bishop Tirechan, both probably written by Tirechan about the year 700.

The student curious to reconstruct the Saint's detailed itinerary in Ireland is always coming up against strange walls of silence regarding certain localities. This happens to be the case with Lough Derg. There is a special reason for those disappointing *lacunae*. The primacy of Armagh was not established without occasional objection. The disciplinary ruling in the eighth century was that every church founded by Patrick himself, or by a bishop whom he consecrated, no matter in what part of Ireland that church was situated, owed dues to the Bishop of Armagh, and had to be prepared to receive him and his retinue, which might number as many as one hundred persons, all of whom had to be suitably entertained. Bishop Tirechan was a strong supporter of the claims of Armagh, but the same cannot be said of all the other bishops of Ireland, and still less of the heads of the great monasteries. These latter exercised a kind of authority over local churches in their neighbourhood, and they would have much preferred that Irish church organisation should be left loosely defined. When Bishop Tirechan was compiling his *Breviarium* he asked the heads of all

the Irish churches to give him details of Saint Patrick's
work in their district. The response he got was disappointing : some sent a laconic refusal ; others just
began to argue against the claims of Armagh. These
ecclesiastics were shrewd men and Bishop Tirechan's
zeal in unearthing knowledge had implications that
they suspected. It was not then a question of Saint
Patrick's honour, which they considered safe (so it is) ;
it was perhaps a question of being prepared to receive
some months later a visit from the Bishop of Armagh
and his retinue of one hundred, arranging hospitality
for them, and undergoing an absolute inquisition to
boot. The reason, therefore, why the modern student
is often so completely baffled has a very human explanation.

Given the condition of affairs, we may be thankful
for any crumb of evidence. It is at least historically
certain that Saint Patrick preached in the district surrounding Lough Derg. Certain details of his movements
in this region are given in the *Tripartite Life* and are
confirmed in the *Breviarium*. The latter document
gives a list of the churches founded by Patrick in the
Barony of Tirhugh, or southern Donegal. Dr. John
Gwynn, annotator of the Book of Armagh, has a note
on this passage from Tirechan, that is very interesting
in our present enquiry :—

> " The route Patrick followed is, in its main
> points, sufficiently determined, from Assaroe (near
> Ballyshannon), north-eastward through the Pass
> of Barnesmore ; then by Ardstraw in Tyrone,
> near Newtown Stewart ; until he crossed the
> Bann at Coleraine . . . ."

Any reader who cares to trace this journey on a map
will agree that Patrick could not have done it without at
least many distant views of the lake. Remembering that
he moved slowly and with an elaborate retinue, drawing
the countryside around him as he went, the probability
that he visited the lake becomes overwhelming.

Moreover, Tirechan says that Patrick founded a church in Tirhugh. Where now is the location of that church? Doctor John Healy, the prolific and well-known writer on early Irish history, believed that the church in question was in the parish of Templecarne. Now, I would not wish it to appear that I am giving Dr. Healy a place as an authority on Celtic history which he himself would not have claimed, and to which he is not entitled. But in this case it happens that no other church in the barony of Tirhugh ever put forward the claim to be of Patrician foundation except the church in the parish of Templecarne. The graveyard of Templecarne is within a couple of miles of Lough Derg on the Pettigo side. Among its ruins are the butts of the walls of an old church. By a process of elimination, this must be the site more or less of the church founded by Saint Patrick in the barony of Tirhugh.

We now have the Saint not merely favoured with distant views of the grey water folded away in the grey hills, but actually doing his apostolic work within a couple of miles of its shore. Here a little digression becomes imperative. Many a reader's impression is completely spoiled by the modern bogey of speed: he has a confused notion of a machine whizzing around the country, just covering ground. The man who is always in a hurry is an excrescence of the twentieth century. Saint Patrick spent thirty years at the evangelisation of Ireland and he did a complete work. He made lengthy stays in each region he visited; he was thorough and deliberate, one of those monumental characters, completely comforting. He examined the Christian possibilities in every district, discovered all the local conditions for his work, made himself master of the situation. Thus, if we can pin him to Templecarne at all, he is safe there for several months. Neither this, nor any other church of Patrician establishment, was " built in a day."

Patrick did not go about his missionary work in Ireland with just a companion or two beside him. His

" household " accompanied him everywhere and it was a retinue just as elaborate as that maintained by later Bishops of Armagh. It usually comprised : an assistant bishop, a chaplain, a brehon, or judge, to advise him in legal matters, a champion, or strong man, as bodyguard, a psalmist, chamberlain, bell-ringer, cook, brewer, sacristan, two table attendants, a chariot-driver, a firewood-man, or provider of fuel, a cow-herd, three smiths, three masons, three artisans, or metal-workers, three embroideresses. A company such as this required an impressive number of vehicles, both chariots and wagons, for the transport of themselves and their equipment.

The churches of that period were built of either timber or just wattle and clay. When Patrick founded a church he nearly always gave a hand himself at the building. His retinue set to work to provide the necessary equipment : his smiths made the nails, door-hinges, handle and bell ; his copper-smith made parts of the altar, the chalice, paten and gospel cover ; his embroidresses provided the vestments and altar linen. While the church was under construction, Patrick preached and baptized in all the surrounding district.

The consecration of the church was a symbol of the work accomplished in that countryside : it meant that Christianity had supplanted the Druid religion. This gesture, however, did not at once liberate Patrick, unless he had among his household someone capable of immediately taking over the new Christian community. If no such candidate happened to be ready for office, there would be a still longer delay in the district while Patrick prepared an assistant priest to take entire charge of the new church.

Patrick's missionary work was carried out with the help of a retinue of the sort described for two reasons : the nature of his work demanded mobile help of that kind ; authority in his day could not be conceived without such a parade of external support. Such a large household must have had many inconveniences, but

Patrick bore with them because they were indispensable. He was no lover of pomp—St. Fiacc's Hymn describes him as being " without sign of pride ". But the lesser kings of Ireland would have had scant respect for any man unable to show the same exterior symbols of power as they themselves affected. So strong was tribal sentiment in the Ireland of the fifth century, any attempt to convert the people without first winning the chieftain's esteem would have been quite useless. Patrick's large household was almost a copy of the retinue maintained by the lesser kings of Ireland and his use of it is one of the many examples of his self-adaptation to native customs in his evangelising tactics.

Like many a lesser man forced to live in the public eye, Patrick's only means of recuperation was an interval of solitude. He was encompassed by people every hour of the day, his personal *entourage* never consisting of less than twenty-four persons. Should members of his " school " (young men whom he was training for the priesthood) happen to accompany him, then the number of his immediate followers might be as many as fifty. He dealt daily with still larger crowds whom he baptized, and throngs of people to whom he preached. Even a saint could not conserve the strength for that kind of work without sometimes renewing it in solitude.

Think of him located somewhere near Templecarne for several months and thus surrounded. The lake would certainly invite him with its promise of refuge and sanctuary. It was inevitable that he should escape to it. The island on which Saint Patrick's Purgatory is now located happens to be the island farthest away from the mainland no matter from what point of the shore it is approached. This is the very island he would naturally choose. He always looked for the most inaccessible place in every district, like the top of Croagh Patrick, enough to daunt the most enthusiastic " fans " ! He had to make sure that he would be absolutely alone. The tradition that he visited this island is continuous since his time, universal in the Irish Church, and peculiarly circumstantial.

B

This is where the legends enter to add their colourful flourish to the plain historical probability. There are current three versions of the same event. One account describes the ancient, dispossessed gods of the Druids (or dethroned devils) flocking northward in retreat as Patrick marched up through the country in his campaign of conversion. A number of those evil spirits had taken up their abode in a cave on Station Island. Grim stories were told of their orgies. The people of the district became so terrified by the evil repute of the place, they would not even look in the direction of the haunted island, and for no price would any man venture to set foot on it. When Patrick arrived in Templecarne, he was told all this. He determined to prove to the people the power of Christ over the forces of evil, and set out alone for that devils' island. The people tried to dissuade him from a venture they considered foolhardy and from which they hardly expected to see him return alive. He took no notice of their warnings, but went over alone to the island where he spent twenty-four hours in personal combat with the demons, whom he routed. This legend makes the island in Lough Derg the site of the final struggle between Patrick and the Druidical power. He returned to the mainland, unharmed of course, and later consecrated Station island as a site of penance. On the neighbouring larger island, called Saints' Island, he founded a monastic settlement which he left in charge of a disciple.

A second version of the legend says that when Patrick reached this district, the people complained to him about a serpent that inhabited the lake and came out at intervals to harm some and terrify everyone. Like one of the Knights of the Round Table, Patrick set off at once for the lake and killed the monster. Its blood dyed the water red, and this explains the name *Loch Derg*, or red lake. For many centuries after this heroic deed the ossified bones of the monster, in the shape of curious rocks, were supposed to remain on the shores of Station Island, in confirmation of the story. Christian art represents the saint standing on the head of a serpent, or with a serpent coiled around the foot of his crozier, in allusion to the belief that he drove out from Ireland forever all snakes and reptiles. The deed is supposed to have been actually performed on Station Island. Anyhow the gesture is more persistently associated with Lough Derg than with any other locality in Ireland.

Yet a third version of the legend describes Patrick's converts as very perplexed by the doctrine of hell and purgatory. He cast about for some means of convincing them. He prayed with fervour on this lake island and then, as if suddenly inspired, traced on the ground with his staff a circle that opened to disclose a pit of fire. When the people saw this miniature hell, they were converted in large numbers. This is said to be the origin of the famous cave on Station Island, which was the outstanding feature of St. Patrick's Purgatory from the very earliest ages until nearly the end of the eighteenth century. A whole *corpus* of European literature has been built up on that cave. It will be fully discussed in a later chapter.

There is a second line of proof, connecting Saint Patrick with Station Island, that obtained from his *Confession*. To my mind it is stronger than that evidence of Tirechan embellished by legend; it is far more fascinating to follow and much richer in consolation. Let it be said first that the *Confession* has emerged with honour from the testing of Higher Criticism, which has not succeeded in casting any doubts upon it as an authentic record written by the Saint himself. It is the most precious document in the whole mass of Irish historical record from beginning to end.

The *Confession* is a simple description of a soul's progress. Even if a reader opened this book determined to disregard the holiness of the writer I think he would be forced to admire the Saint Paul-like qualities revealed in every line of that writing. There is expressed in it a simple manliness, an unbending strength of mind, a capacity for love, for physical endurance, and for faithfulness which could not fail to touch even the most cynical mind. It was the Roman, Patrick, who gave the Irish character its permanent stamp. The national ideal of manhood, in its purest and of course unattainable form, is described in the *Confession*.

Patrick's simple creed of life was that some kind of " chastening " has to be undergone before one can hope for any spiritual enlightenment :—

> " After we have been chastened, and have come to the knowledge of God, we shall exalt and praise his wondrous works . . . . "
>
> " I remained in death and in unbelief until I had been chastened exceedingly, and humbled in truth by hunger and nakedness, and that daily . . . . "

As a boy, when he was brought to Ireland a captive slave, he had had a stern initiation into physical hardship, loneliness and humiliation, in other words, the necessary " chastening " :

> " Now, after I came to Ireland, tending flocks was my daily occupation ; and constantly I used to pray in the daytime. Love of God and the fear of Him increased more and more, and faith grew, and the spirit was moved, so that in one day (I would say) as many as a hundred prayers, and at night nearly as many, so that I used to stay even in the woods and on the mountain (to this end). And before daybreak I used to be roused to prayer, in snow, in frost, in rain ; and I felt no hurt ; nor was there any sluggishness in me . . . . And there verily one night I heard in my sleep a voice saying to me, ' Thou fastest to good purpose . . . . ' "

When Patrick became a missionary he did not change the means which, as a boy on Mount Slemish, he had found powerful in gaining God's help : solitude, endless repetitive prayer, vigil, fasting, physical endurance. He used the same means to fight Druidism and to free from the slavery of sin the Irish people to whom he himself had once been enslaved.

Austerity as the keynote of Patrick's character is emphasized, too, by the biographer Fiacc, already quoted in another connection :—

> " He sang a hundred psalms every night . . . . He slept on a bare flagstone with a wet mantle around him, a pillar-stone was his bolster ; he left not his body in warmth . . . . "

The Celtic Christians closely imitated Patrick and soon became famous in western Europe for their asceticism. They held that a Christian's life on earth is a warfare, and that the flesh has to be mortified if the spirit is to be free. Vigil, or denying sleep to the body, was a penance highly favoured, and a cave such as that on Station Island was just what would be suitable for the purpose. They held that fasting gave power to prayer. The twice-quoted Fiacc himself was wont to retire into a cave for Lenten penance, a practice also common among the British and Scottish saints.

Their method was to turn prayer into a kind of ascetical exercise, almost a physical endurance test. Here is a counsel of Celtic Christianity :—

> " Thy measure of prayer : till thy tears shall fall.
> " Thy measure of genuflexions : till thy sweat come often."

The Celtic saints believed in the endless repetition of long vocal prayer as a means of forcing the soul to life, the body as well as the mind being compelled to share in this effort by continual genuflexions, or by keeping the arms extended in the form of a cross, or by long kneeling. They favoured the prayer *Beati immaculati* because it is the longest of the psalms. From the ranks

of the apostles, they singled out James the Less for
special devotion and called him "Iacob glunuck"
("James of the Knees") because his knees were said
to have become the size of a camel's from perpetually
kneeling in prayer. This is the kind of little detail that
the Celtic Christians hailed with enthusiasm : they felt
they knew that kind of man.   Spiritual strength was
attained only by stern self-discipline. The body had to be
immolated. There was no compromise.

Kenney, the famous American authority, who has
collected together so many of those fascinating details,
suggests that the insistence on vocal prayer was due to
the Celtic monks being "less capable of concentration
than the Easterns."   This seems to me extraordinary
comment. It is quite clear from Saint Patrick's *Confession*
that he had reached the mystical heights, attained the
Unitive Way, practised the Prayer of Quiet, call it
what you will. He taught that which he had experienced ;
all his disciples took the same road to God. Real concentration of the will and the intelligence is just what they
insisted on.   They formalised the method for concen-
trating, so that fake contemplation became virtually
impossible.   Time spent in mere moods of devotion
they would never have permitted.   They were among
the hardest realists the world has ever known. All that
pious slobber, that religious grimacing and simpering,
with which we are so sadly familiar in the twentieth
century, they would simply have dismissed as just
not Christianity at all. And note at least one result of
their method : they were quite untroubled by heresy.

Every pilgrim to Saint Patrick's Purgatory has to
undertake a three days' penance.   It is the hardest
Christian pilgrimage in the modern world, including as
it does a three-days' fast, one all-night vigil, compulsory
walking barefoot on stones, and endless repetition of
vocal prayer.   But as this was the method of Celtic
Christianity, the centuries are here telescoped, and the

fifth can be lived in the twentieth with refreshment to the mind. I think Christendom could be challenged to produce a more striking instance of continuity.

I wonder does it happen anywhere else in the world that the atmosphere of a place calls to life a character, or that its mere routine reconstructs a person ? This is what happens at Lough Derg. In that red-eyed combat with sleep in which pilgrims must engage, in their three-day struggle with the " noontide devil " of hunger, in their burden of fatigue, in the discomfort of walking barefoot over sharp stones, in the inescapable weariness of long prayer, they come face to face with Patrick. His authentic voice becomes audible. Strong and in-eluctable, he is there.

It is certain that Saint Patrick personally evangelised southern Donegal. He founded one church there, probably identical in site with the graveyard at Templecarne. He must have known the lake and the probability that he visited some of its islands becomes overwhelming in view of the strong, unbroken tradition concerning Station Island. His *Confession* finds a living illustration to-day in the Island practice, and nowhere else in the Irish Church. The " way " that he taught and practised is perpetuated there in a manner that, without him, defies rational explanation. He who submits to that discipline discovers that he is touching a live chord of communication with Celtic Christianity.

II. LOUGH AND ISLANDS

LET us leave history for the moment and turn to topography for variety's sake. I invite the reader to take with me an excursion around the lake. In pre-Christian times it is said to have been called *Finn Loch*, or the Fair Lake. One tradition, already alluded to, says that the name was changed to *Dearg*, or red, when the water was dyed crimson with the blood of the serpent slain there by Saint Patrick. However, a more plausible and scientific explanation is that there are innumerable iron springs in the lake bed and on the surrounding shore, adding their rusty trickles to the water, which might well account for the reddish-brown hue it sometimes assumes.

The antiquary, John O'Donovan, on the other hand, dismissed the name, Loch Dearg, and corrected it to *Loch Derc*, meaning the Lake of the Cave. This opinion finds a good deal of modern support. The name Loch Deirc would seem to confirm the view that even in pre-Christian times the cave was held to be the central feature of the place.

Professor MacNeill, foremost modern authority on the Celtic period, has an original opinion. He holds that the ancient name of the lake was *Loch Gerg*, meaning " Lake of the Grouse, the oldest bird sanctuary on record ! " However, as the evidence for none of these derivations is conclusive, the reader is free to make his own choice among them.

Lough Derg is dotted with forty-six small islands, some of them graced with shrubs and occasional rowans, or ash, but the greater number are only bare rocks projecting out of the water. In addition to Station Island and Saints' Island, there are Friars', Bilberry, Ash, Allingham, Kelly's, Goat, Derg-More, Dearg-Beg, Eagle's Rock, Trough, Philip Boy, Gavelands, Stormy,

Bull's Islands, and several other nameless ones, the resort of sea-gulls and water-fowl, whose cries are almost the only sounds that break the silence of this deserted region.

Friars' Island is unmistakable, because it is the nearest to the ferry. Unfortunately, the origin of its name is unknown. It rises higher out of the water than the others and the mound in its centre is crowned with a group of fir-trees. These mark the site of a curious improvised graveyard, where lie a number of victims of a tragic boating accident that took place in 1795.

The largest island in Lough Derg is Inishgoosk ; it has no historical interest. The second largest is Saints' Island, called St. Dabheoc's Island in early Christian times. It lies two miles north-west of Station Island, is some ten acres in extent, and it contains the largest area of fertile soil among all the lake islands. The verdure of its surface and the traces of ancient tillage still to be seen attract attention even from afar. We shall disembark at this island, but first let us find out all we can about Saint Dabheoc, who gave it its first name.

He was a disciple of Saint Patrick, probably a very youthful one, as he lived for fifty-five years after Patrick's death. He came from Wales in the apostle's train and was probably not a Celt, but a foreigner of good birth. He is said to have been son of a British lesser king, and grandson, on his mother's side, of a Saxon king. All his family followed him to Ireland in due course and became converted to Christianity.

Dabheoc was the first Abbot of whom we have record in charge of the monastic settlement on Saints' Island ; his monks took over the care of the penitential cave on Station Island, where a few of them always lived. The parish of Templecarne, in which Lough Derg is situated, used to be called Termon-Dabheoc, or Dabheoc's patrimony. There is a Dabheoc commemorated no less than three times in the Calendar of Irish Saints : on January 1st, July 24th, and December 16th. If it is the same individual always, he must have been greatly honoured.

He is listed as one of the Twelve Apostles of Ireland in
the legend that describes the cursing of Tara. The
historian, Colgan, says that Dabheoc had the gift of
prophecy, which enabled him to describe the coming of
Columcille. There is a reference in *Loca Patriciana*
to the fact that he paid a visit in his extreme old age
to the monastic school of Ardstraw, where Saint Kevin
was then a scholar.

At any rate Dabheoc enhanced the fame of Lough
Derg, which became in later ages a place of local pilgrimage in his honour. From allusions in the book of
Giraldus Cambrensis, it is evident that his name was
widely invoked and revered as late as the thirteenth
century. In this connection, it is perhaps of some interest
to add that a handsome variety of heather, called Saint
Dabheoc's Heath, flourishes in the west of Ireland.

There is a great boulder called Saint Dabheoc's Chair
on the summit of one of the low hills on the western
shore of the lake. It is still marked in modern ordnance
maps. In a dry season, this height is best approached
from the lake by landing at a point half-way between
the rock called Saint Brigid's Chair and the little creek,
Portcreevy. One must then climb in a direct line to the
top of the hill, where the seat may be readily identified
by a cairn-like mound and a deep pit, or trough, beside
it. Curiously enough, this " chair " faces south with
Lough Derg completely hidden at the back of it and,
in front, a panorama of rich country lit up by angles of
Lough Erne.

Turning back from this Seat to look down on Lough
Derg, the aerial view of Station Island is exquisite. I
was once so rewarded on a Spring morning—a memorable
experience. The air was balmy, wine-like, bog-filtered,
the silence broken only by the occasional trilling of larks.
It happened to be a very colourful day, rare in this region.
Rolling, tawny bogland framed the blue water teased
into darker ruffles by the sportive April winds. Down
below, Station Island rose up in imperial grandeur
against its background of low hills. These were con-

tinually swept by shadows as the sun played hide-and-seek with the clouds, lighting up transient shades of delicate colour on the landscape. The green-domed Basilica and the buildings so tightly clustered around it might have been floating on some miracle raft. It was hard to believe that they had any anchorage. As unsubstantial and unreal as a mirage, one was afraid to look away lest they should vanish. On the distant hills, one could just discern the white gleam of some houses. Otherwise there was no trace of man, no roads, no sign of cultivation anywhere. There stood the Basilica proclaiming its message to an empty world. If Saint John, the Beloved Disciple, was granted visions on the Isle of Patmos, one could easily credit Dabheoc, too, with having had experience of some unrecorded apocalypse above the shores of Lough Derg.

But such a climb as I have described from the lake shore is impossible except during a long, dry season. When the weather is broken, this mountain slope becomes a morass, denying foothold. The more usual approach is by road. Suppose the traveller is proceeding from Pettigo to Lough Derg on the main road, he will come upon the road to Saint Dabheoc's Seat branching away to the left, about a mile from the lake shore, a thatched cottage at the junction of roads being a convenient landmark. It is a narrow road, very steep in places, and so stony throughout its length that it is a trial to the most willing motor-car and an ordeal to any driver. On the first mile, one disturbs the privacy of several cottages, being forced to skim close to their gable ends and stone wall crofts, with the risk of upsetting their cooking and washing utensils, usually left standing about outside the doors. Later, the road breaks free from all human habitation and strides off boldly for the bog, in the middle of which it comes to an abrupt and disconcerting end. The traveller in quest of Saint Dabheoc's Seat should not follow this road to its inexplicable end. He should leave it at the last house on the righthand side, and then climb the hill at the back of this dwelling, taking a

north-easterly direction. When the lake swings suddenly
into his view, he will find the Seat without much difficulty.
It is in fact the only remarkable stone on the hill-top.

Archaeologists, however, and most tourists, are warned
that Saint Dabheoc's Seat may disappoint them. It is
only a rough natural formation. There is not even a
crudely-carved stone there, nor any embellishments of
man, there is not even a rag on a bush. It is the forgotten
memorial of a forgotten saint. Apart from the view,
there is nothing to compensate the explorer except the
subtle reward of " atmosphere." In the clear, ex-
hilirating air of that remote high ground, where the
silence is so profound it almost assails the ear, one
arrives at a new appreciation of men of Dabheoc's kind,
whose soul found peace only in such solitudes.

Dabheoc's name is commemorated, too, in Seadavog
mountain, a low peak to the west of his Seat on the
southern shore of the lake. Seadavog was likewise the
ancient name of the townland from which this mountain
rises. Ballymacavanny is its modern name, but Seadavog
still clings to one small part of the townland, its western
end.

Returning to the lake shore, another notable landmark
there should be considered, Saint Brigid's Chair. It is a
large rock, roughly-shaped like a high-backed chair, and
it is prominent even among the large boulders surrounding
it. Viewed from a boat on the water, the Chair stands out
sharply against the vandyke brown of hibernating
heathers and the orange of wilted bracken. A few almost
needleless pines, old and lonely, stand sentinel on the
slopes above it. The base of the great rock is in the
water. There are no marks or carvings on the stone.
It is a comfortable, roomy seat, perfectly smooth, with a
sloping back. There is, however, no documentary evidence
that Saint Brigid ever visited this locality. The rock was
originally known as Saint Dabheoc's Chair, probably
down to the seventeenth century, at which period Saint
Brigid's name was first attached to one of the cells on
Station Island and probably also to this rock. An un-

usually complete view of Station Island may be had
from it. Local tradition has it that Saint Brigid sat there,
gazing at the Island, while waiting for a coracle to take
her over.

The question of the ownership of Saint Brigid's Chair
presents a pretty legal problem. The late Sir John Leslie,
of Glasslough, Co. Monaghan, used to be the landlord
of all this countryside. During the present century,
the Catholic Church re-acquired the ownership of Station
Island and the necessary strip of land around the ferry
on the mainland. When the larger estates of Ireland were
divided up in recent years, the Irish Land Commission
took over the shores of the lake, but the lake itself still
belongs to the Leslies. The rock known as Saint Brigid's
Chair rests half on the shore and half in the water.
Who owns it ?

To return now to Saint Dabheoc, although we know that
he was tremendously important in his own day, we have
no detailed knowledge of him. He was placed in charge
of the Celtic monastery on Saints' Island at some date
not determined, and governed it until his death in 516.
He is said to have been buried in the abbey there, a
building which was destroyed by the Danes. We know
the names of only two of his successors on Saints' Island :
Cillene (who died in 721) and Avil.

From the death of its first Abbot in the year 516
until the onslaught of the Danes about the year 836, we
know nothing of the history of that monastery on Saints'
Island. It was Celtic Christianity's Golden Age. There
were no foreign invasions, and Ireland was disturbed by
nothing more serious than internal conflicts between
rival princes. Celtic civilization during that period got
every opportunity to blossom from its Patrician seed. It
was in the sixth century that the fame of Clonard, Clonfert, Bangor and Clonmacnoise spread through Europe.
Columcille carried Christian culture to Iona in 563. Then
Aidan took the Gospel southwards, and Lindisfarne
became an offshoot of Iona ; Saint Gall evangelized
Switzerland ; Saint Fridolin, the Rhine country ; and

Saint Cataldus, southern Italy. Saint Columbanus spread the Celtic concept of Christianity by establishing monasteries throughout France, southern Germany, Switzerland and northern Italy. Such names as Luxeuil, Bobbio and Ratisbon denote outposts of Christian colonisation by Irishmen. It was an age of unrivalled missionary expansion, never again to be repeated. As Saint Bernard expressed it, " swarms of saints poured out as though a flood had risen." At the Court of Charlemagne, there were Irishmen described as " incomparably schooled in human learning."

But even if we have no historic details of the monastery on Saints' Island during that Golden Age, we can still form a very good idea of what it was like. There is on record a detailed description of at least one such Celtic monastery, that of Columcille in Iona, written by a contemporary, Adamnan, in his well-known life of Columcille. This description could, in a manner of speaking serve for all. I do not say, of course, that Saints' Island ever reached the same splendour as Iona ; it was certainly always on a much smaller and more modest scale.

A Celtic monastic settlement did not resemble the later cloisters of the great contemplative orders. Its purpose was different. It was never considered a retreat from the world. It was an operating base for bringing the gospel to the surrounding country. Numbers of those who lived in the settlement were not in ecclesiastical orders at all. Guests received special attention.

This is what Iona looked like : a large group of small buildings, surrounded by an enclosing wall, or vallum. The church was the most important building in the group. The next in order of dignity was the Abbot's house, usually a little apart from the others and sometimes on a slight elevation. There was one main pathway cutting through the enclosure and giving access to the other buildings, namely : the kitchen, pantry, (a separate hut housing the domestic utensils, baskets, water jars, and pots) ; guest-house, library, artificers' workshops ; a smithy, a carpenter's shop, a corn-mill, a storehouse for venison and fish, a granary, a barn, cow-stalls, a kiln, a game store and a general larder. The monastic settlement on Saints' Island must have had a general lay-out resembling this, but of course it had only the buildings necessary for a small community's needs on a small island.

The community included a prior, scribe, lector, anchorite, butler, baker, cook, smith, brazier, carpenter, janitor, all of whom were usually in holy orders. Other members of the community who had no orders might include a brewer, clothier, embroiderer, and firewood-man.

Early in the ninth century, an ominous cloud appeared in the north, which was presently to overcast all such fair scenes as that presented by Saints' Island. The Danes began their devastating raids on the shores, rivers, and even the inland lakes of Ireland. One after another, the great monastic groups of the country became their prey. Saint Dabheoc's monastery shared the fate of the others ; its rich and germinative life was quenched by the marauders. We have no details. There is a brief entry in the Four Masters under the year 836, stating that all the churches of the neighbouring Lough Erne were destroyed by the Danes in that year. Saints' Island was probably included among them. The Danes not only levelled buildings, but they destroyed documents, too, which explains why this island's history cannot now be bridged between the death of Dabheoc and the coming of the Augustinians. The Danish assault on Saints' Island must have totally ruined the place beyond hope of any immediate resurrection.

We have no details of that Danish sack. But there was about the same time a very similar monastic settlement on an island in Strangford Lough, County Down : Nendrum, on Island Mahee. Nendrum's history, too, was completely broken in 974, when the Danes landed there. Nothing was known of what happened, except that some of the monks succeeded in escaping ; all the members of the settlement who were caught were killed, and the buildings were either set on fire, or they caught fire during the sack. But the Belfast Archaeological

Society have carried out a supremely successful work at Nendrum, proving that even yet the past can be recovered through determination and patience. They excavated with great skill and care the formidable ruins on Island Mahee and they were rewarded beyond the wildest hope. They uncovered clear evidence that a fire, a massacre, and a flight of the inhabitants had taken place before the deposit of centuries covered up the ruins. They were able to identify the school-house. It had evidently been roofed with wooden beams over which straw had been laid. Charred wood and straw were found in the débris and even nails that had held the roof beams in place. Writing tablets of slate, or stone, and iron styles for writing, were found on the floor of this building, just as they had dropped from the hands of the pupils, when the alarm was given. These pathetic tablets are now preserved in the Belfast Museum, the designs on them still plainly visible : a triquetra, a spiral, a Celtic decoration design, a letter of the alphabet, even a humorous drawing of a horse half-seated, evidently the work of a pupil in a frisky, or whimsical mood. The bell was found buried in a corner outside the church where the monks in their headlong flight had apparently paused to hide it. All those finds, with their living associations, are in a separate case, labelled " Nendrum " in the Belfast Museum. The curator is only too willing to unlock it and allow the enquirer to touch the objects on the shelves. This is one way to meditate on the end of the Celtic glory on Saints' Island. It is impossible to take that Nendrum bell in one's hands without emotion. It is Mochaoi's bell, but it could so easily have been Dabheoc's.

The first chapter, then, of Saints' Island history is probably lost forever. But Adamnan's admirable description of Iona provides us with a very good idea of what it was like. And the discoveries of modern archaeologists on a contemporary island settlement, Nendrum, give us at least a fleeting insight into its probable pathetic close.

Three hundred years after the sack of the Danes, this monastic life on Saints' Island arose again, phoenix-like, from its grave. Religious life went on there until it was assailed by the Reformers in the seventeenth century and by them destroyed for the second time. As in the case of Island Mahee, before the excavations were carried out, there are now on Saints' Island two distinct classes of ruins, one super-imposed over the other, all impenetrably sealed by the slow accretion of centuries, which have deposited upon the stones their inextricable growth.

I remember a strange Easter Sunday spent on Saints' Island, not indeed with any hope of finding archaeological confirmation of its history, but simply in communing with the past. Neither the Celtic monks, direct heirs to Dabheoc, nor the Canons Regular of Saint Augustine, who succeeded them, celebrated the Resurrection there that morning. No Alleluias were sung in Paschal gladness, there were no tiers of candles, nor banks of bright flowers. A melancholy silence shrouded the scene, broken only by the occasional mournful cries of aquatic birds. It was Easter Sunday only for furtive wild animals, heedless winds, rank vegetation, and the enormous pillows of moss characteristic of this sward.

The island lies near the western shore of the lake, so close that at one time there was a foot-bridge connecting island and mainland. The remains of the stone piers that once supported this bridge can still be seen on the lake bed when the water is very still. The island is oval (described locally as " goose-egg ") in its shape ; it rises to a hump in the middle and it is edged with sallies nearly all the way round.

The land was cultivated at one time. The marks of the furrows were clearly to be seen at the early season of which I speak. The east end, from which the remains of a little quay jut out, is now completely overgrown.

C

There are signs of rats and rabbits (though these small animals do not usually flourish together), but of no other living creature. Everywhere underfoot there was a carpet of the deepest moss, imposing additional silence. The air was warm, balmy and rejuvenating ; unconcernedly the Easter sunshine poured down on that scene of desertion and decay.

The " ruins " are not even worthy of the name : just shapeless mounds smothered in vegetation and butts of walls submerged in moss and nettles. I had been warned to visit the site early in the year, because after May the island cannot be traversed, so dense becomes its vegetation. In the height of summer, no trace whatever can be seen of the ancient monastic settlement and pilgrims' hostel, as by then the weeds have become waist-high. But in spring, while growth is not yet far advanced, one can see the fragments of stones marking the rude graves in the cemetery, and one can trace the outline of at least a large enclosure which was probably the church.

Do not visit Saints' Island with expectations of finding carved stones, a clear ground plan of ancient buildings, or examples of early Christian masonry. There is nothing of the kind to be seen. You will find instead only stumps, bumps, and conquering armies of weeds, cruel in their strength. Pillaged now of whatever memorials it once had, the island has only a few trees scattered over its surface : rowans and hawthorns, not remarkable except that they are thickly draped with green-grey lichen ; no holy well could have its surrounding bushes so festooned with rag-offerings as are those hoary trees with their lichen garlands. For the rest, briars are in possession, loping unchecked almost from end to end of the island, to the exasperation of archaeologists, who indeed have shown a distaste for this venerable, but forbidding, ground. Even the famous antiquarian, O'Donovan, gave it only scant attention.

Ferns, mostly of the lady-fern variety, grow abnormally thick at their bases here, forming a stalk which gives them a most unusual appearance. There is also a thick spread of nettles. Rushes, too, growing in great robust masses, obliterate all traces of a sacred past as completely as Cromwell himself might have desired. On prizing up a few loose stones, one exposes heaps of enormous bluebell bulbs, white and skull-like in shape. Shortly after our visit, the island must have been veiled in the smoky-blue of their profuse florescence. Moss, too, has proved itself a great ally of the persecutor, smothering the level stones as though eager to complete their obliteration.

There is an additional reason for the complete absence of remains on Saints' Island. Since it ceased to be occupied, the practice grew up of removing stones from it, a custom that has been carried out for hundreds of years. Numbers of those stones were used to mark graves in Templecarne churchyard. Lest readers should hope to discover anything about the island with the help of stones removed from it, I may be pardoned for making a digression at this point. I, too, had that hope and was deceived. A long search of Templecarne graveyard in an effort to identify certain stones that had been removed by local families from Saints' Island proved fruitless. The graveyard on this historic site is of course immensely old, overcrowded beyond description, and extremely badly kept. Here, too, the stones are blanketed with moss, or jealously concealed by tough grasses. There is a small Celtic cross, with a quarter of the circle missing, evidently of ancient design, which is said to be one of the many memorials taken away from Saints' Island. I managed to prize up out of the grass in Templecarne graveyard the shaftless cross, locally described as the " churndash," which used to mark the grave of pilgrims drowned in that boating disaster of 1795. Now that even this cross is detached from its base, there is no finding the grave it used to mark.

Returning to Saints' Island, sadness is its keynote. Nothing but grief and disappointment await the pilgrim who goes there in a spirit of reverent curiosity. There are no traces left to exalt the heart, nothing to inspire pride in the past, no consolation in the possession of remains devoutly preserved, no comfort in knowing that retribution was made for the wrongs of other times. Here is the very desolation that the spoilers desired : the lone cry of the curlew replaces the chant of the monks, weeds triumph over religious rites. Since the aggressors levelled those monastic walls with their pick-axes and crowbars in the seventeenth century, there has been no recovery on this ground.

We exposed many stones on Saints' Island by dragging off their covering of moss and tearing away the grasses. All we discovered was that the buildings were of the primitive, dry-masonry variety. The stones were but rudely dressed to present an elongated flat surface. The upright stones in the graveyard are bare of inscription and innocent of even the most elementary carving.

A well-planned surface fire would do much towards restoring this ground to its last sad condition when its buildings were levelled by the seventeenth century soldiers ; and that state of charred surface would at any rate be preferable to its present condition as the passive and abject victim of parasitic vegetation. If, by good fortune, this island ever again became ecclesiastical property, such a beginning at restoration might be made.

In the midst of this desolation is an enclosure thickly overgrown with briars, to which barriers of nettles almost prohibit entrance : this is said to be the site of the original Celtic monastery. A mound within it is pointed out as Saint Dabheoc's grave. This was the bitterest moment in our voyage of exploration, for the holy place where Dabheoc rests is the most abandoned and inaccessible in the whole island. Briars encompass it so thickly, and with such aggressiveness, one cannot approach within five or six feet of the mound. Such is the reputed burial place of the first Abbot of Lough Derg.

III. MEDIAEVAL FAME

THREE hundred years of the history of Saint Patrick's Purgatory appear to have dropped out of human knowledge. The first phase of its recorded history, meagre though it is, ceases when the Danes destroyed the Celtic monastic settlement on Saints' Island in the ninth century. Its second phase opens when the Canons Regular of Saint Augustine took up the charge of the pilgrimage in the twelfth century.

The exact date when the Augustinians went to live among the monastic ruins on Saints' Island is not known. Lough Derg was constituted a Priory dependent on the Abbey of Saints Peter and Paul in Armagh sometime between the years 1130 and 1134. The Augustinians' arrival at Lough Derg must be placed between those years. They were probably brought there by Saint Malachy, Primate of Armagh, as that great reformer established numerous houses of both Cistercians and Canons Regular everywhere throughout Ireland. It is certain that the Augustinians were securely in possession of the Lough Derg sanctuary by the year 1135.

What was happening on Station Island during that hidden interval of three hundred years ? We know nothing except that the pilgrimage went on without interruption. The Augustinians did not have to revive it. On the contrary, it was such a popular devotion, they had to go and live on Saints' Island in order to take charge of it. During the closed period of three hundred years, priests must have gone over with the pilgrims so as to give them the Sacraments. But this was not enough. It was necessary to have resident priests on the adjacent island, too.

Who were the Canons Regular of Saint Augustine who succeeded the Celtic monks ? As an order, they were a kind of golden mean between the more severe monastic groups and the secular clergy. All the Celtic monks were not priests, but every member of the Canons Regular was in Holy Orders : that was the principal difference between the two fraternities. The Canons lived a monastic life in community, but their rule was not half as severe as that of the Celtic monks. Three hundred years had passed. The Canons suited the religious trend of the time : they were modest and unassuming in their way of life and moderate in their mortifications. They happened to be in tune with the spirit of the century that witnessed their revival. As hospitality to pilgrims and travellers was a notable feature of their vocation, they were specially suited to the work on Saints' Island.

From the moment the Canons take possession of Lough Derg, a great amount of information about the pilgrimage becomes immediately available. The contrast with the preceding centuries of silence is so strange, it has led many writers into the error of dating the origin of the pilgrimage from the twelfth century. The truth is that the Canons were entirely faithful to their charge in fostering the devotion handed over to them ; in doing so, they collected and perpetuated all the traditional lore concerning that devotion. But to say that they either invented it or initiated the pilgrimage, is simply preposterous.

The Augustinians were in possession of the sanctuary for about twelve years, when it became almost suddenly famous in Europe. This happened through the accident of one pilgrim from abroad, who claimed to have had an extraordinary experience in the penitential cave, and who managed to have his story committed to writing. His account was copied, re-copied again and again, and diffused throughout Europe. To the mind of the mid-twelfth century, it was a good story. A whole *corpus* of European literature, a truly amazing tissue of fantasy and fable, was build around that tale. Every new addition to the story seemed to bring yet another notability from abroad, eager to investigate and then add his tithe of evidence to the toppling tower of illusion and dreams.

The pilgrim responsible for bringing this tide of pilgrims from abroad, who kept the pens of scribes so busy, was only a poor soldier of fortune, called the Knight Owen. His name, too, appears deviously in mediaeval manuscripts as Owain, Miles, Ennius, Ennio, Owein, Oengus, or Oenus. His visit to Lough Derg probably took place in 1147. The date is calculated by the detail that he followed up his penance on the island by joining a Crusade to the Holy Land during the reign of King Stephen, and this expedition dated from 1147 to 1149.

The soldier, Owen, would not have been capable of writing down his own story. But when the Crusade ended, he went back to England. There he chanced to meet the superior of a Cistercian monastery in Ludlow, who offered him a little job of work that would probably be to his liking. The Cistercian had just been given a grant of land in Ireland and had been empowered to open there a new house of the order. He was about to send over for that purpose one of his monks, named Gilbert. The monk could not travel alone : he needed a companion who would act as guide, interpreter and, if necessary, body-guard. The Knight Owen knew Ireland and he agreed to go with Gilbert.

Gilbert soon discovered on the journey that his travelling companion was no ordinary soldier of fortune, but a man stamped by a profound religious experience. Gradually the monk won the soldier's confidence, and was told the whole story of a life unusually sinful, that was dramatically changed by a miraculous conversion. The soldier arose out of this experience an utterly different man, who became completely absorbed in repentance and who tried to make reparation for a number of years in several different countries. The climax of his conversion came in Ireland, in Lough Derg. Still devoured by a thirst for penance, he had undertaken the pilgrimage and was led, as was customary, into the cave of penance to remain there and keep vigil for twenty-four hours. But when the Knight Owen was left alone, he saw the after-life ; he struggled with demons and was consoled by angels ; he walked through Hell ; he was admitted to the portals of Paradise. When the Prior and monks came to release him at the end of his vigil, they found him half-dead and had to carry him from the cave.

Is it true ? The question is completely irrelevant. Owen, at any rate, succeeded in convincing his monk companion, Gilbert. When the latter eventually got back to his monastery in Ludlow, he could talk of nothing else. His brethren were mostly incredulous, and the topic was beginning to die down when another little incident occurred to give it fresh impetus. A cleric from Ireland happened to turn up in Ludlow. His name was Florence ; he was probably Florence O'Carolan, who became Bishop of Derry in 1185. The monks told him Gilbert's story and he listened with sober interest. He confirmed that there was a place of pilgrimage in Ireland such as Owen had described, that it was on a lake island, where there was a cave said to be of fabulous origin, in which one had to keep a vigil of twenty-four hours. The discovery of this kernel of truth in Owen's story revived great interest in it among the Ludlow community. Finally, one of the monks wrote down the whole story just as he had had it from Father Gilbert. He signed his manuscript " *Fr. H. monachorum de Saltereis minimum.*" It was the chronicler, Mathew of Paris, who concluded that the letter " H." stood for Henry. Since his time, that author who called himself, " least among the monks of Saltrey " has become known as " Henry of Saltrey." The name, however, might equally well have been any one of a dozen names beginning with H.

This anonymous religious author, "Frater H.", is less shadowy in his own way, as an impersonal recorder, than Father Gilbert, of whom we know practically nothing, or even the Knight Owen, hero of the story. The manuscript reveals to some extent the author's personality. It is obviously the writing of a serious person, who was anxious to set down in writing that which he had heard on good authority. He makes no pretence to literary ability. He begins by explaining the series of events that induced him to write down the story. He is consistent all through in his rôle of impersonal narrator. He is emphatic that he has invented nothing. He wrote in the passionate belief that the story should be put on record and made widely known. Incidentally, he thus fulfilled one of the essential conditions of literature.

No doubt the humble author would have been astonished if he could have foreseen the immediate, enormous and abiding popularity of his work. The human mind's appetite for excitement, that to-day is appeased by detective fiction thrillers and the film, seized with avidity on the monk of Saltrey's story. It was eagerly copied and re-copied. It became in a short time the best known of all mediaeval romances. Manuscripts, or fragments of them, dealing with the story, still survive in all the principal libraries of Europe.

The image of the pale-faced soldier penitent, who never smiled, and who could not refer to his terrifying spiritual experiences without painful emotion, became known all over Europe in the twelfth and thirteenth centuries. Thousands of rapt listeners to that story shared in the deep impression it had made on its first hearer, Father Gilbert.

Owen's repentance had been as impressive as his sins had been terrible. Beyond darkly indicating a murky past, the monk of Saltrey gives no details of the misdeeds that had stained the chevalier's soul. These details were obligingly supplied at a much later date (1627) by the Spanish writer, Juan Perez de Montalvan. This individual cites no authority for his very detailed account. With all due apologies, therefore, I now put it before the reader merely as a curiosity for what it is worth.

The Knight Owen (or Luis Ennius as he becomes in

de Montalvan's language) was born in Ireland. His mother died at his birth. His father afterwards took him abroad and died in Toulouse, when Owen was about fifteen. The boy had been allowed to run wild from his childhood but, when he was left without control of any kind, he turned into a precocious criminal.

He became a mercenary soldier and gambling was one of his many weaknesses. One night, he was playing with a companion, a sergeant-at-arms, when some squabble arose between them concerning the play. Owen knocked out the light, overpowered his companion, robbed him in the dark and made his escape. The authorities were then on his track and he had to remain in hiding. He had only one remaining relative in the world, a young cousin named Theodosia, and she was a nun. He went to her for sanctuary. The convent agreed to shelter him, on account of his good family name, until the hue and cry should have died down. The soldier completely abused this kindness. He talked his cousin into allowing him into the convent enclosure at night-time and then he robbed the place. After that he persuaded Theodosia to run away with him. The cousins escaped overseas to Valencia, where they settled down to have a good time. The money, however, came to an end and Owen was not capable of earning sufficient to support them. He bullied Theodosia into leading an infamous life so that they could both live on her gains. This girl, however, had been troubled with qualms of conscience nearly all the time. She ran away from him the first chance she got and took refuge again in a convent. She was admitted as a servant and remained with the nuns until her death six years later.

Owen followed her, but found that his power over her was gone. She refused to go back with him and he could not shake her determination. After that he became completely reckless. One night, he made up his mind to murder a man in order to get his money and he prepared an elaborate ambush for the victim. He had to wait there in hiding for a long time. As he waited, he saw a piece of paper fluttering in the air before him. He tried to grab it, but it evaded his grasp, luring him to run after it. The moment he left the ambush, the man whom he had been waiting to kill passed on his way, unharmed. The very same thing happened the following night, and still the supernatural nature of the incident did not occur to Owen. On the third night, with murder still in his heart, he succeeded in seizing the paper as it hovered within his grasp. According to the Spanish writer's rather confused account, there was depicted on the paper a corpse, with Owen's name written under it in large letters. Impressed in spite of himself, Owen looked up from the paper and saw in the air before him a cross outlined in light, and under it the words : " Here a man was killed. Pray to God for his soul." Grace suddenly flooded the outlaw's heart. He went on a pilgrimage to Rome, where he confessed and did penance. Afterwards he returned to Ireland and, still harried by the desire for reparation, he went to Lough Derg to make satisfaction for his sins by prayer and fasting.

The Lough Derg pilgrimage was a great deal more exacting then than it is now. A fast of fifteen days was compulsory as a preparation for a vigil of twenty-four hours which the pilgrim had to spend locked up alone in the little cave. It is a relief to put away the highly-coloured account of the Knight Owen's early life, written by Juan Perez de Montalvan, and go back to the sober prose of Brother H. of Saltrey. This is the latter's account of what happened to the penitent soldier during his vigil in the cave. He walked boldly forward through the intense darkness and presently perceived a thin pencil of light which guided him to the exit. Outside, " there was only such light as is visible after sunset in Winter." He saw a hall enclosed with pillars and arches like a monks' cloister and, going in, he sat down to admire its beauty. Then fifteen youths, dressed in white, came in. One of them explained to Owen that the tortures of Hell were to be shown him, and that, should evil spirits attack him, he could save himself by invoking the holy name of Jesus. When his kindly mentors had gone, the knight waited with all the fortitude he could muster. Suddenly, the tumult of hell irrupted in his ears. It was noise so overwhelming, so savage, so intolerable to the human ear, he said that had he not been so fore-warned he would have lost his reason. A multitude of deformed demons surrounded him, jostling him with derisive laughter. With jeers, mockery and lies, they tried in every possible way to turn him back. Finding him determined to press forward, they raced gleefully to kindle a fire before him, then seized and bound him despite his struggles, and flung him into the flames. As the fire bit his flesh, the soldier called on the Holy Name and at once escaped. All his subsequent experiences were marked by the same tension and extreme sense of peril. He wandered through the dreary plains of a penal region, reeling back again and again before the tortures he was compelled to witness. The climax came when he saw a river of fire winding sluggishly through a land-scape of nightmare. This river gave off flames and foul fumes ; souls were writhing in it. The only means of crossing it was by a bridge, so high, so excessively fragile and slippery, that to attempt it seemed madness. Once more invoking the Holy Name, Owen committed himself to the perilous passage and escaped, the demons raising behind him a disappointed howl so unendurable to the human ear that it seemed to him the worst of all the pains he had had to suffer. On the other side of the bridge, the portals of an earthly Paradise opened to receive him. All the trembling mortal's senses were then bathed in divine refreshment : music and song to assuage his outraged hearing, suave odours in his nostrils, a cool air, a golden light, flowers and fruit. Then he saw a great procession of the saved with joy on their faces, robed in cloth of gold, green, purple, hyacinth, blue and white, the nature of the dress indicating the merit and rank of the wearer. He made a gesture to join this happy company, but was turned back and told that his days of exile on earth were not ended. He retraced his steps then,

passing quickly again through the purgatorial regions.
This time, at his reappearance, the devils fled terrified
through the air and did not address him. He regained
the Cave just as the Prior arrived to unlock the door for
him.

The mediaeval historians accepted without question
the story of the Knight Owen and incorporated it in
their chronicles : Roger Wendover reproduced the
Saltrey text, with alterations, in his *Flores Historiarum*,
from which it was taken by the celebrated Matthew
Paris for inclusion in his *Chronica Majora*. Again,
Ralph Higden inserted it in his *Polychronicon*, in turn
re-copied by John Bompton in his *Chronicon*. The
poetess, Marie de France, gave the story poetical form
in Old French. Several versions of it were written in
Old English.

Further impetus was given to the spread of the Knight's
story about the year 1275, when the Italian chronicler,
Jacobus de Voragine, included it in his famous *Golden
Legend*, one of the most popular religious works of the
thirteenth century and, incidentally, among the first
group of books to be printed. In Voragine's version,
the pilgrim's name is given as Nicholas instead of Owen,
but otherwise the account tallies generally with that of
Henry of Saltrey. By the year 1500, there were in
circulation seventy-four Latin versions of this work as
well as innumerable versions in English, French, Italian,
German and Bohemian.

It is claimed that even the great Dante was indebted
to the Saltrey manuscript. All Irish writers who touch on
this subject, however, are inclined greatly to exaggerate
that indebtedness. It is true that the Saltrey manuscript
and the Comedy present us with much similarity of
ideas. The two men were sent on their voyage among
the dead by divine agency. Both had to share for
a fleeting instant in some of the tortures they
witnessed. We are confronted in the two writings with a

whole succession of almost identical episodes : extremes of heat and cold ; the dreary plain, dotted with pits of fire ; souls in burning tombs ; the river of fire giving off sulphurous fumes ; souls transfixed with stakes to the ground, or preyed upon by reptiles ; the perilous bridge ; finally, a kind of terrestrial Garden of Eden and a procession of the saved. There are even phrases of great similarity in the Saltrey manuscript and in the Comedy.

But it has to be remembered that the fiery pits, the pools of ice, the river of fire, the perilous bridge were the stock-in-trade of that whole cycle of visions preceding Dante's work : the Voyage of St. Brendan, the Vision of Fursey, of Adamnan, of Tundale, of Turkill, of Alberic. If Dante did indeed take some ideas from the Saltrey manuscript in particular, it forms only a thin thread in the tangled skein which he found, unravelled, and then wove again into the pattern of his own work. Much of the raw material Dante used is saved from oblivion only by the Comedy's splendour ; the sources are naïve, incoherent and infantile when compared with that monumental work.

No serious literary comparison is possible between Dante's Comedy and the Saltrey writing. The difference between the two works would make such a comparison an impossible feat : one is a volume and the other is a leaflet. One work is a discussion of the whole Christian scheme of redemption, the other is just a colourful description of a vision.

Dante, as most readers know, described in his Comedy the states of Purgatory, Hell, a kind of terrestrial Paradise (ante-chamber of Heaven) and Paradise itself. The Saltrey manuscript, on the other hand, describes a state of punishment which is both Purgatory and Hell, and a terrestrial Eden. The real problem posed by the Saltrey manuscript is that it makes hardly any distinction between Hell and Purgatory. To modern ideas, its horror is the horror of Hell. Demons there have complete license to torture souls. There is no hint of consolation, or hope that the punishment will end. The only

clue given that it is not the nethermost pit is that the
Holy Name prevails over the demons ; they scatter
when it is spoken.

There is no resemblance, then, between the Purgatory
described in the Saltrey manuscript and that detailed
by Dante. Dante includes all the souls in Purgatory
in the Communion of Saints and invests them in an
atmosphere of love, patience and hope.

Later poets than Dante enhanced the marvellous
story, making Lough Derg the focus of the whole Christian
world as a site of supernatural visions. In Ariosto's
chief poem, *Orlando Furioso*, he mentions the fabulous
cave in Ireland, where mercy and salvation abound
for sinners, listing the pilgrimage among the " deeds of
daring " (*l'audaci imprese*) which a knight in that age of
chivalry would normally undertake. As the theme of
Ariosto's poem is Christian honour, the inclusion of
Lough Derg has a special significance. The poet expressed
the popular European idea of the pilgrimage. Geographi-
cally remote and obscure as was that lake island, yet a
visit to it ranked with joining a Crusade or some other
such valorous enterprise which it then behoved the ideal
knight to include in his exploits.

The fascination of the story spread to Spain and, in
time, became responsible for a chapter in Spanish
literature. Pedro Calderon de la Barca, dramatist of the
seventeenth century, found inspiration in the Knight
Owen's story. He wrote a religious drama in verse,
St. Patrick's Purgatory, which was considered worthy to
be performed in the Royal Theatre in Madrid. An
English metrical translation of this work was made by
the Irish poet, Denis Florence MacCarthy, in 1847.

The most remarkable illustration of Lough Derg's
European fame in the later Middle Ages appears in the
heading of a letter written by Saint Catherine of Siena.

It is worth giving this incident in some detail in order to show what the pilgrimage to Lough Derg had become in the popular European mind some two hundred years after the visit there of the Knight Owen.

The caption of the letter reads as follows :—

"To Don John, a Carthusian Monk in Rome, who was tried by temptations, and who wanted to go to St. Patrick's Purgatory, and when permission to go there was not granted him, became sorely afflicted in his mind."

Clearly there is quite a story behind a letter with such a caption.

Like nearly all this saint's letters, this document, too, deals with a crisis in the life of the person to whom it was written. Don John's difficulty can be reconstructed between its lines. Whatever form his "temptations" took, they had shaken him badly. Their onslaught had been powerful enough to make him dread a recurrence. He believed that only some rigorous form of penance could save him from a repetition of the ordeal. The Lough Derg pilgrimage seemed to his sick soul the one haven in the Christian world where his mind could recover its health. He applied to his superiors for permission to go to Ireland. Showing no sympathy for his state of mind, they refused him leave to go, thus callously abandoning him to his wretchedness, or so it seemed to him.

He fell into a state of profound dejection, alternating with moods of rebellion, in which it seemed likely that he would leave his Order and give up his vocation. The affair brought him to a crisis in his religious life ; he suffered fits of terror and despair, aggravated by his frayed nerves. All because he had not been allowed to undertake the pilgrimage to Lough Derg ! Imagine, then, what this devotion had begun to seem to the religious mind of Europe : an absolutely certain antiseptic for every known suppuration of the soul ! Don John's brethren pleaded and reasoned with him, as they saw even his physical health affected by his mental misery.

Finally, the Carthusian visitor brought the whole matter before Saint Catherine, begging her to write to Don John.

The young Dominican saint tried to deal with this unusual affair and quell the trouble that had arisen among the Carthusians. She wrote about the year 1372, being then twenty-five. She had a grasp of moral theology that was purely intuitive and was gifted with a torrent of fiery eloquence. Lovingly, she puts these at the service of the distracted priest. She wrote him nearly two thousand words.

She makes no comment whatever about the Patrician shrine that so powerfully lured the poor Carthusian monk in Rome. Her silence seemed to imply that it was all he believed it to be : a unique haven for tortured souls. She does not discuss the suitability of the place for his special spiritual trouble, because that was not really the point at issue. She knew well that even the stern discipline of Lough Derg would not cure Don John's spiritual weakness. With her usual incisiveness she goes to the root of the matter and reminds him of his vow of obedience. If he could only look at his supposed grievance in a supernatural light, she tells him that his difficulties would immediately vanish.

She dwells on the " temptations " from which he so longed to be set free, repeating the axiom that there is no sin unless the will consents : no matter how the soul is disturbed by grievous thoughts, provoked by the devil or by creatures, no matter how the weakness of the flesh humiliates the spirit, so long as the will remains steadfast, not consenting to the mind's abasement but ashamed, the soul emerges stronger from such struggles.

She then proceeds to look at obedience from every angle. The obedient man, she said, never trusts to his own judgment, which he suspects is faulty. On the contrary, he completely surrenders himself to his Order, believing firmly that God will enlighten his superiors in all that concerns his salvation. Even if his superior happens to be an utterly stupid man (an *idiota* is

D

Catherine's word), with every kind of human failing and hopelessly dense, yet the obedient soul will not be shaken in his trust. The man who is obedient does not obey in one way only as it pleases him, or in one place, or time, but he obeys in everything, everywhere and always. He is never scandalized, no matter what he is told to do. He is patient about the restrictions imposed by his Order. When he does not get his own way, he does not sink into dejection, but he rejoices.

Catherine tells the Carthusian that, in reality, his chief affliction is his own stubborn will. Therefore he will never find peace until he gets the better of himself, and casts out his obsession with what she calls "holy hatred." Never afraid to use the hard word when it is necessary, she says the disobedient man is simply a fool (*un semplice*). She insists that Don John's idea is nothing more than a delusion of the devil. She concludes by saying : " Bow your head to obedience and stay in your cell. Guard against doing your own will as you prize the life of your soul."

It is a tribute to Lough Derg and evidence of its pre-eminence in Europe that, in the Italy of the later fourteenth century, the devil could use its renown to trouble even the souls of the elect.

IV. CAVES AND FANTASIES

THE Knight Owen's story became so popular in Europe that it gave rise to a good deal of misunderstanding about the penitential cave on Station Island. It raised dangerous hopes. The possibility of conversing with the dead, or even seeing them again, had the same fascination in the Middle Ages as it has to-day. People believed the cave was an entrance to the other world, and that one might see there one's beloved dead and perhaps receive some " message " from them. Men crushed under the tragedy of bereavement heard of Saint Patrick's Purgatory with morbid eagerness and pondered on it with desperate longing. The difficult journey to that inaccessible lake island, the preliminary prayer and fasting of fifteen days did not intimidate them, when they thought they had a chance of thereby piercing the veil of the unknown.

St. Patrick's Purgatory thus became credited with mysteries and marvels which the guardians of the site would probably never have claimed for it. One must bear in mind that the authorities in charge of the sanctuary had really nothing to do with the belief expressed by foreign pilgrims that marvels and apparitions were a sure occurrence there. Still less of course did the Church give any sanction to this belief. The Irish people themselves were always level-headed in their view of the place. According to them, one went to Lough Derg to do penance and hope for grace—nothing more. It was a foreign pilgrim who first spread the tale of having seen visions there and it was chiefly foreigners who believed him.

The fame of Lough Derg in literature was followed by a rush of distinguished pilgrims from all parts of Europe, who visited the lake island in an unbroken stream from the beginning of the twelfth to the end of the fifteenth century. The Purgatory became the recognised venue also of " hard cases," or notorious sinners from abroad, who could show a crime record equal to that of the Knight Owen. Irish pilgrims, however, still held to the original concept of the place as one that gave the ordinary man a chance to do penance. The foreign idea of the sanctuary was exciting and fantastic, the native one was wholly spiritual.

All the evidence goes to show that the Irish Church disliked the fantasy vogue and tried to combat it as it grew. At one time a ruling was made that no-one from abroad could enter the Purgatory without a signed permit from the Primate of Armagh and the Bishop of Clogher. Dissuasion soon became a recognised part of the ritual for entry to the cave. The Primate tried to dissuade the pilgrim ; so did the Bishop ; so did the Prior of the Purgatory. All this was peculiar. The discouragement seems to have been tried only on the foreign visitors, who came so obviously primed with expectation of marvels.

Among Irish pilgrims who are said to have visited the island in the twelfth century the most noteworthy was Tiernan O'Rourke, Prince of Breffni. It is the historian Keating who tells the story that O'Rourke made the pilgrimage to Lough Derg in 1152. During his absence, his wife, Devorgilla, sent a message to Diarmuid MacMurrough of Leinster, telling him that the coast was clear, and they then arranged their elopement, which was a prelude to the Anglo-Norman invasion. O'Rourke belonged to the continental category of pilgrims, inasmuch as his sins were scarlet. He outrivalled any Dane as a despoiler of churches and a plunderer of monasteries. Whether or not he ever really did penance on the holy island, it is certain that he had a spiritual account to settle.

One of the most famous pilgrims who followed in Owen's wake was a Knight of Hungary named Georgius Crissaphan. He, too, had been a great sinner. Before he reached the age of twenty-four he had committed murder two hundred and fifty times. But he experienced conversion and gave up his career as a soldier in order to become a hermit. In the year 1353 he made up his mind to seek for the graces reputed to be found in Lough Derg, " at the ends of the world in Ireland." He did not come in state with a retinue, as did other notable pilgrims. He chose rather to make the journey on foot, walking through Gascony, Navarre, the Kingdom of France as it then was, across to England and so to Ireland. When he had thus laboriously arrived at the Augustinian Priory on Saints' Island, a great disappointment awaited him. He had not known the ruling that no-one was allowed enter the Purgatory without express leave from the Primate of Ireland and, in addition, a written permit from the Bishop of the Clogher diocese. The Hungarian Knight had to retrace his steps and walk back to Armagh, a journey that took him eight days. In due time he returned to Lough Derg with the necessary permits.

At that period, the twenty-four hours' vigil in the cave had to be preceded by confession, penance and a fast of fifteen days on bread and water. Having complied with all those conditions, Georgius was admitted to the cave where, like Owen, he wandered through the regions of the dead. The prominent feature of his experience was the number of messages he brought back for all the rulers of the earth, including the reigning Pope, the Soldan of Babylon, the Kings of England and France, and the Primate of Ireland! In order that no-one could doubt him, an archangel gave him " most sure and secret signs unknown to mortal except to those to whom George was sent."

Accounts of St. Patrick's Purgatory became ever magnified in the telling. We find it described by foreigners as a dreadful pit emitting flames day and night ; as a cavern swept by icy blasts from the nether world ; even as a mountain of sulphur continuously burning. There is soon no limit to the terrors with which imagination was willing to credit that remote island site.

Lough Derg was visited in 1358 by a French penitent

called Louis de France, or Louis d'Auxerre. His experiences in the cave outrivalled, if anything, those of the Hungarian Georgius, but they are worth a separate comment for their novelty. The Frenchman's account had all the flavour of the Troubadours' romantic songs. Women of incredible beauty, dressed like queens and crowned with precious stones, tried to tempt him. He encountered them sitting in the shade of a lovely tree in a great field, innocently playing chess. One of them thus disarmingly addressed him :—

> "O Knight of great constancy and valour, I felt in my heart a strange and abiding joy at your coming amongst us, for I love men who are daring and of fame for constancy."

Even in the fourteenth century, however, not everyone was carried away by the fantasies. There were level-headed pilgrims, too, among whom such tales provoked only amused scepticism. Froissart, in his *Chronicles*, relates that, during a visit to England, he questioned one Sir William Lisle about the famous cave in Ireland. Sir William told him that he and another English knight had not only seen it but had made the vigil there. In reply to Froissart's eager questions, Sir William's account was very tame. When the door was locked behind them—he said—they sat on the stone steps leading down into the cellar and thought they noticed a hot vapour coming up against their faces. They were overcome by sleep and slept profoundly all night. Both of them had fantastic dreams, not to say nightmares, but in the morning when they came out, they could not recollect those dreams. Therefore Sir William was very sensibly inclined to dismiss the whole business as imagination.

And yet the wonder-seekers and marvel-finders were ever more numerous than the sceptics. Two years after Froissart's enquiry, that is in 1397, the Purgatory was visited by a terrific grandee, a Spanish Count named Raymond de Perelhos, who was attached to the court

of Pope Benedict XII at Avignon.   Count Raymond
did not seek out the Purgatory in order to rid himself
of the guilt of heinous crimes, but expressly to get into
communication with his sovereign, King John of Arragon,
who had just died.   Raymond had the Pope's permission
to make the pilgrimage, and he carried a safe-conduct
from King Richard II of England which he presented
to the Viceroy in Ireland, the Earl of March.   March said
everything he could think of to dissuade the pilgrim,
pointing out that he " had to make a long road and pass
through lands of savage people, who had not a way of
life of a kind to which anyone should trust himself."
Finding the pilgrim determined, however, he resignedly
passed him on to the Primate.   This priest did his best,
too, to dissuade Count Raymond and, when he failed,
he transferred him to Niall Og O'Neill, King of Ulster,
for safe-conduct to the island.   Raymond stated afterwards that the Primate of Armagh gave him for his
protection through the O'Neill territory " a hundred
soldiers armed in their manner to accompany me . . .
and another interpreter."

This pilgrim's experiences were as hair-raising as
Owen's or those of Georgius and Louis de Sur.   He
succeeded in meeting the shade of his late sovereign.
However, when he asked the king the reason why he
had been condemned to Purgatory, he received only an
evasive answer.   Raymond was surprised to meet there
also a kinswoman who was alive when he began his
journey and of whose death he had not heard.   She was
less reserved than the king.   She told him why she was
punished : for having spent so much time " in trimming
and painting her face."

One might be tempted to attribute the greater part
of those marvels to the alleged vivid imagination of the
Latin races, if it were not for another contemporary
account (1409) of one William Staunton, a staid native
of Durham in England.   He was cheered at the very
beginning of his wonderful experience in the cave by
encountering therein his own patron saints, John of

Bridlington and Saint Ives. He met his sister and the man she loved, and his sister upbraided him soundly for having prevented their marriage in the world. This pilgrim's account of St. Patrick's Purgatory equals all the preceding stories in variety and fantasy of scene.

Staunton was followed in a couple of years by yet another Hungarian Knight, Lawrence Rathold, who made his way to the little island in the Donegal lake. Rathold, too, was among the " believers." He had an original reason for probing the secrets of the cave : he wanted to rid himself of certain doubts on Faith that were troubling him ; human curiosity, too, entered into his motives. When challenged to say whether he saw his visions bodily or spiritually, he cautiously quoted St. Paul on the third heaven : " Whether in the body or out of the body I know not, God knoweth." Rathold added that in his case it was probably " in the body " because of the prosaic detail that he took nine pieces of taper into the cave with him and burned them all, one after another, before he came out again.

What is one to make of it ? To dismiss the whole thing as imagination is the easiest way to be rid of it, but the puzzle is not so easily solved. The universality and the persistence of the testimony that visions occurred at Lough Derg is disturbing to the most determined common-sense. It went on for so long, for four hundred years, and the witnesses came from every walk of life and from so many countries : England, France, Spain, Italy, Hungary. The cases cited are only some of the written accounts that have survived and were collected in a random way. Admittedly, some penitents may have wanted to explain their own enlightenment on the enormity of sin, and a convenient way to do it was to put the homily into the framework of a vision at Lough Derg. This device might dispose of some of the accounts, but not of all of them. It is something unique in human history that so many witnesses came from so many different points of the compass over such a long period of time and all agreed in their main contention that they saw a vision.

The last mentioned pilgrim, Lawrence Rathold, was accompanied to Lough Derg by a most useful companion (from our point of view), a Florentine merchant named Antonio Mannini, whom we have to thank for an exact description of the cave as it was in the year 1411.

> " The place is three feet wide, nine feet long
> and high enough for a man to kneel but not to
> stand upright. It is exactly like a sepulchre, for
> it is vaulted overhead and lies towards the south,
> that is, there is a niche about three feet long in the
> direction of the chapel, in which the Prior had told
> me to remain and wait, saying my prayers the while."

Contrast that sober and exact description with the impression of vast size conveyed by H. of Saltrey's original account :—

> " Trusting in God, [Owen] walked alone through
> the cave, the darkness growing more dense, he could
> presently see nothing. At length, towards the end
> of the cave, he saw a pencil of light . . . . "

Contrast it again with the extravagant description of the cave given by Georgius in 1353 :—

> " Which entrance is a very deep pit of two miles
> and more with gradually twisting steps as are
> customary in the ascent or descent of belfries."

Mannini, whose prosy description would win the approval of modern scientific archaeologists, was reticent about his visions. While not denying that he had been favoured in the usual way, he refused to disclose the nature of his experience.

One is grateful to Mannini both for his reticence and for his accuracy of description, for in truth those tales of wonder grow a little monotonous, each teller's imagination seeming to be allowed free rein. Having accompanied a dozen or more of those pilgrims, the reader's receptive faculty becomes somewhat blunted. Even the most sadistic description of punishment,

ranging from immersion in boiling metal to having one's
entrails devoured by serpents, ceases to provoke a
twinge of horror. Even the foretaste of Paradise glimpsed
at the end of the journey becomes, through repetition,
faintly wearisome. We feel we know it all : those fields
of light where the atmosphere is crystal clear and filled
with suave odours, where fruit and flowers abound,
the city paved with gold, walled with jasper and precious
stones. The variations on the theme have all been
sounded. This harmless and to some minds, edifying,
branch of devotional reading appears to have had its
zenith of popularity, but tastes change and the vogue
has come to its inevitable end.

Caxton, (translator and pioneer of printing), in the
account added to his translation of the *Mirror of the
World* (1480) marks a stage in this change of taste.
His approach would be described in modern jargon as
the " debunking " process. He says :—

> " It may well be that of ancient time it hath
> been thus as afore is written . . . ., but I have
> spoken with diverse men that have been therein.
> And that one of them was an high Canon of Water-
> ford, which told me that he had been therein five
> or six times. And he saw nor suffered no such
> things. He saith that with procession the Religious
> men that be there bring him into the Hole and
> shut the door after him and then he walketh
> groping into it, where as he said there be places and
> manner of couches to rest on. And there he was
> all the night in contemplation and prayer and also
> slept there ; and on the morn he came out again.
> Otherwhile in their sleep some men have marvellous
> dreams. And other thing he saw not."

There is the simple, unvarnished account of an Irish
pilgrim as opposed to the extravagant fantasies of
the overseas visitors. This unnamed " high canon of
Waterford " sounds like an average honest Christian
who went to the island many times for the same reason

that thousands of men and women go there to-day, that is, to make a spiritual retreat in an inviting solitude, where prayer can be pointed by fasting, vigil and penance.

There are, as might be expected, some good ghost stories connected with Lough Derg. A certain Count Raymond served in one of the last of the Crusades towards the end of the fourteenth century. One day, during an engagement, his life was saved by a companion in arms, an ordinary soldier of fortune named Ugolino. The two men became very good friends after this episode. When the Crusade was ended, they travelled to Europe together, and Raymond invited Ugolino to his home. The visit was a very happy one for a while, but then serious trouble arose. Raymond had an only sister, Madeleine, and she and Ugolino fell in love. The family would not countenance the affair : they were noble ; Ugolino had neither birth, nor means, nor a profession to recommend him. The usual kind of discouragement was tried, but without success. One day Raymond himself tried to remonstrate with his sister for what he considered her unfair encouragement to his friend. Madeleine, as is the way in such affairs, was completely unreasonable. A scene ensued between brother and sister, and Raymond, in an access of rage that he could not control, stabbed her. She died as a result of the wound, and Raymond fled.

He was immediately harried with remorse for what he had done and almost at once decided to travel in the direction of Lough Derg, where he thought he might have a chance of making reparation. After many vicissitudes, he came to Ireland and at last crossed the Donegal mountains and came within sight of the holy island. It was late evening and the boatman told him it was too late to go across that night, that he had better wait until morning. Count Raymond settled down to spend the night as best he could in a rudely improvised shelter on the shore.

Meanwhile, Ugolino, too, had to fly from the murdered girl's home. But he took with him the bloodstained dagger, swearing to be revenged. All that fine comradeship between the two men had now turned to bitter hatred. Ugolino followed the Count, sometimes losing track of him for days on end, but always catching up again on his traces. He did not actually overtake him until the very night that Raymond was waiting on the shore of Lough Derg. There was a sharp and brief encounter, which ended in Raymond meeting the same death as his sister and with the same weapon, at the hands of the soldier who had once saved his life. For many decades afterwards, a ghost in foreign attire used to be seen pacing around the island in the evening.

The second story is not so tragic. It concerns the Knight, Don Diego Riaz, who was both a great sinner and a great penitent. He set out from distant Peru to do penance at Lough Derg, bringing with him one attendant. Illness overtook the Knight on that long journey and he died on the way. His regret was so keen at not having been able to reach Lough Derg that his servant promised, as a consolation to that death-bed, that he himself would do the pilgrimage for the repose of his master's soul. The faithful servant was as good as his word. When at last he reached the lake and was being rowed across to the island, Don Diego appeared in the boat, took a hand at the oars and disappeared when the island was reached. This story is incorporated in a poem by Thomas D'Arcy M'Gee.

There arrived at Lough Derg in 1494 a most important pilgrim from abroad, whose investigation of the cave was to mark the end of an epoch in the history of Saint Patrick's Purgatory. He was a Canon Regular of Saint Augustine attached to the monastery of Eymstadt, Holland. His name is unknown. He is always described in record as the Dutch monk, or the monk of Eymstadt.

He is represented as a very holy man, who found himself more comfortable than he wished in the Eymstadt monastery. He applied for permission to transfer to some other order where the rule was stricter, or alternatively, for leave to travel the world as a mendicant friar. For a long time his superiors tried to reason him out of taking this step, probably feeling that he had been inspired rather late in life by the Franciscan ideal. But at length this nameless Augustinian had his way and quitted both Eymstadt and the security of the monastic life. In due time, he turned up in Ireland, where he sought out St. Patrick's Purgatory, eager to penetrate its mystery. He made the usual mistake of going direct to the Prior, who explained that no-one was allowed enter the cave without permits from the Primate and the bishop of the diocese. The pilgrim had to retrace his steps back to Armagh.

It is now that the Dutch pilgrim's report becomes so markedly different from all other accounts. He went first to the bishop and, because he was travelling in the guise of a mendicant, he says that he found it extremely difficult to get access to him. It is impossible to trace the inaccessible prelate, because the See of Clogher was vacant at that particular time. The Dutch monk must have gone either to the vicar capitular, or to a neighbouring bishop. Whoever this ecclesiastic was, he demanded money for the permit, and the monk answered that he was penniless and that, anyhow, to charge for such permits was simony. After considerable difficulty, he got the necessary document and went on to the Primate. Here he had the same difficulty : a bad reception, a long wait, and then a demand for money. Finally, the Dutch monk got back to Lough Derg and, for the third time, money was demanded from him, this time by the Prior, for the privilege of entering the Purgatory. Once again he had to point out that this demand was equivalent to simony. Finally, after a great deal of argument, he was admitted to the cavern.

He sat all night in the darkness, trembling with fear as he waited for the demons to pounce on him. Nothing whatever happened. He saw nothing, heard nothing, and suffered nothing beyond the chill discomfort of his vigil. But he seems to have become exceedingly annoyed by morning.

He probably did not know the momentum with which that tale of wonders had spread itself throughout Europe in the face of Irish discouragement. His experience of the place did not at all come up to his expectations. He decided the whole thing was a piece of trickery bolstered up by the natives merely as a money-making scheme. When he left Ireland, he proceeded to lodge a complaint with Pope Alexander VI. An investigation was made, with the result that the ex-Augustinian triumphed. He was sent back again to Ireland, carrying a Papal Order that the cave should be closed up.

Three years after the Dutch monk's disappointing vigil in the cave, this Papal Order was carried out. About the feast of St. Patrick in the year 1497, the cave was dug up and filled in, the Primate of Ireland, the Bishop of Clogher and the Guardian of the Franciscan Abbey in Donegal being present. These witnessed in writing to the cave's destruction and sent the document back to Rome by the same busy monk who had brought the Papal Order.

The reasons given for closing the cave are curious, but unsatisfactory to the student. First, let us take the Dutchman's assertion that the devotion gave rise to simony. Even if it were true that the Primate, the Bishop and the Prior were accustomed to receiving a fee from each pilgrim, this practice does not fit the theological definition of simony. Anyhow, all record goes to show that Irish ecclesiastical authority in the Middle Ages tended to discourage foreigners at any rate from making a vigil in the cave. It is difficult to know how too frequent requests from abroad to visit the Purgatory could be discouraged other than by dissuasion and by levying a toll on the issue of permits. If the Irish Churchmen were mostly concerned with getting revenue out of the pilgrimage, it has to be said that they were bad businessmen !

Moreover, the pilgrim of that age spent fifteen days on the island, during which he was given at least bread every day ; he had the advantage of special religious ceremonies for his individual needs ; he enjoyed every spiritual help that the monastic guardians of the sanctuary could give him. It seems only reasonable, then, that he should contribute something towards the upkeep of the monastery.

To the student of the Purgatory's literary and historical record, this querulous complaint about fees comes as a complete surprise. Not only is it the first time any such complaint arises, but it is the first time there is even mention of money in the records. Up to this point, one has always felt a certain sympathy with the successive Primates of Armagh who must have been sometimes greatly bothered by those peregrinating notabilities from abroad. Take the Count Raymond de Perelhos, for example, whose grandeur was such that it had to be safeguarded by the Primate with no less than one hundred armed soldiers and an interpreter !

The Four Masters say nothing about the closing of the cave, which should have been a matter of concern to the whole of Ireland. The *Annals of Ulster*, however, record the event under the date 1497, and assign a totally different reason for the Papal Order than that already discussed :—

> " It being understood by everyone in general from ' The History of the Knight ' and other old books that this was not the Purgatory Patrick got from God although they were, everyone, visiting it."

This is interesting comment. The cave that had been closed up, then, was not that precious cavern on Station Island, which had been the Mecca of foreign pilgrims for so many hundreds of years. The Dutch monk had never been admitted into the right cave at all, after all

the acrimonious argument ! For some reason that cannot
be easily determined, the pilgrimage authorities, previous
to the Dutch monk's visit, had ceased to take pilgrims
over to Station Island for the vigil, but had opened for
that purpose a cave of their own within the monastery
enclosure on Saints' Island. It must have been an
attempt to re-order the pilgrimage practice in a manner
more convenient to themselves. This explains perfectly
why the Papal Order had been so rapidly and completely
carried out. The cave that had been filled in was only
a substitute cave on Saints' Island and the Primate
and the Bishop looked on at its destruction with
equanimity. I think it would not have been so easy
even by Papal Order to get the real cave on Station
Island dug up and filled in.

The facsimile cave in which the Dutch pilgrim had been
incarcerated with such annoyance to himself cannot
have been long in use, certainly not long enough to
give its adoption any kind of traditional standing.
Sixty years before the Dutch monk's visit (that is, in
the year 1434), a Knight of the Golden Fleece named
Guillebert de Lannoy had made the Lough Derg pilgrimage. It is unmistakable, from the description he
left of his experience, that the Priory of the Augustinians
was on one rather large island in the lake (Saints' Island)
and that the cave, site of the Purgatory, was on an
adjoining small island (Station Island).

The edict suppressing the pilgrimage did not remain
long in force. The same *Annals of Ulster* which record
the closing of the cave in 1497 describe the visit of a
French pilgrim only nineteen years later, that is, in 1516.
The following year (1517) the Papal Nuncio at the Court
of King Henry VIII, Francesco Chiericati, describes a
visit to Lough Derg in a letter to Isabella d'Este. He
says that he did not make the pilgrimage himself, but
that he accompanied two other pilgrims, through motives
of curiosity, and watched them go through the prescribed
devotions. The Nuncio looked through a book kept in
the church at that time, in which the names of all pilgrims

were recorded. Another point of interest is that by this date the pilgrimage had already been reduced to a nine days' fast as a preparation for the twenty-four hour vigil in the cave.

Where was the cave when the Nuncio wrote of it—in Station Island, or Saints' Island ? Clearly the vigil was again being kept in the original, traditional and authentic cave on Station Island. The substitute cave on Saints' Island, filled in by the order of the Pope, had never been re-opened. By 1522, the ruling Primate of Armagh having made strong representations to Rome, Alexander VI's Bull of Suppression was recalled. Later in the same century, the pilgrimage was favoured with Papal indulgences.

Notable mention of the Purgatory was made by the Jesuit martyr, Edmund Campion, who travelled in Ireland in 1570 and wrote its history. He did not visit Lough Derg, but he discussed it with several people, and made his own intelligent conclusions :—

> " I met a priest, who told me that he had gone the same pilgrimage and affirmed the order of premises : but that he for his own part saw no sight in the world, save only fearful dreams when he chanced to nod and those he said were exceedingly horrible . . . . "

The tale of visions, however, had run its course even before the visit of the censorious Dutch monk. It was over. The world had altered now and popular taste had changed. There was to be heard no more of that *skritching shrill from dungeon lugge*, or fearsome howling from a dark cavern, as quoted by Holinshed in his *Chronicles*. But if the Purgatory was losing its renown for visions, its pre-eminence in the Christian world as a place of penance remained unchallenged.

E

V.   THE IRISH WAY

HERE were two schools of thought about Lough Derg, as already explained : one foreign and excitingly fantastic ; the other native, sternly realistic, purely spiritual.   Here, then, is the converse of the picture described in the last chapter : the reflection the pilgrimage found in Irish letters, with special reference to Gaelic bardic poetry.

The earliest of these poems is that attributed to Donnchadh Mor O Dalaigh, who died in the year 1244. He belonged to the generation immediately following that of Brother H. of Saltrey.   Supposing the Knight Owen really were an historical personage, O Dalaigh could have known people who had spoken with him. This poet flourished just as the vision-cycle was beginning its meteoric course.   He is sufficiently close in time to the origin of the whole affair to make his views extremely interesting.   He is, moreover, commonly conceded to be the greatest religious poet of his period, " one who never was and never will be surpassed," say the Four Masters.   All his poems that have come down to us are religious in theme.   He wrote what is to our knowledge the earliest extant poem in Irish on Lough Derg.   The theme could not fail to attract him.   We turn eagerly then to his poem.   Did *he* see the after-life ?   What has he to say about it ?   Nothing whatever that is in the least sensational ; absolutely nothing.

O Dalaigh says that he had gone to Lough Derg to weep over the Passion of Christ and now grieves because his eyes are tearless.   He asks God in tones of real poignancy for the gift of tears, for sorrow like Patrick's. He says that the cold and the fasting he has to suffer are really too good for his body, so hardened in sinfulness, and that he is deeply ashamed of himself for going through the pilgrimage rite with a heart as hard as a stone. The number of times this poem was copied leads one to believe it was a favourite, that it won applause and was judged a success. This man, whose name was one to conjure with among the scribes of his generation, was seemingly not the only Irish pilgrim whose exciting " reward " at Lough Derg was a bewildering sense of dryness and desertion, a conviction that not Patrick only, but God Himself, had vanished from the universe. The belief expressed by O Dalaigh in a mood of exalted spirituality is precisely that to which the modern pilgrim aspires (often vainly, of course) : the gulf of seven hundred years is bridged by a spiritual unanimity that is absolute.

The next poem in this group is three hundred years later in time. It was written at a date when the fantasies concerning Lough Derg had made their indelible impression on European literature. Tadhg Dall O Higginn was born probably about 1550 and died in 1591. He was the poet of O Conor Sligo and his people were fairly large land-owners. Recognised as probably the most typical representative of his class, the *filidh*, O Higginn's output consists mainly of elegies, complimentary addresses, satires, inaugural verse and other purely professional compositions. He is said to have died a violent death at the hands of the O'Hara clan because he had so castigated the family in a satire, calling them " six thieving vagrants, ragged and poverty-stricken " who had repaid his hospitality to them by stealing from him even the very milk for his household. The evidence for this story, however, is not very strong.

O Higginn did well in his career as poet because (final test from the Irish viewpoint) he died possessed of considerable land in his own right. His view of Lough Derg may be taken both as that of the ordinary people and—in particular—as that of the ruling classes in the Gaelic polity, who were his patrons.

He describes the holy island as a house of healing where every wound of sin can be perfectly cured. The healer there is Patrick, " noble and generous," " the beloved prophet of the Irish "; he is the doctor to whom one can surrender with complete trust, certain of relief. Without Patrick, the Gaels are like the crew of a ship when their captain is wounded. He calls the cave the sinner's " bed of healing," the only place of sojourn he covets. He will leave his misfortunes (meaning his soul-sickness) behind in it. He will come out of it cured. It is a dark, gloomy cave, but the cures that are wrought in it make it, spiritually speaking, the brightest haven in the world.

A contemporary of Tadhg Dall O Higginn's, as well as a namesake, was the Younger Feargal O Higginn, who wrote a poem on Lough Derg about the year 1570. He says he has made up his mind to go into Patrick's cave to be " cleansed of his wickedness "; and that God left Patrick's " splendid guidance to Ireland " to enable the Irish to deal with original sin.

Tuileagna Mac Torna O Maolchonaire was another pilgrim poet contemporary with the above-named. He was average in every way, neither a great sinner nor conspicuously religious, nor even a purely religious poet. We read of him that he was " pardoned " on the 17th March, 1584, with the usual sequel of a grant of land, so that evidently he had thrown in his lot with the conqueror. He was from Kilkenny and wrote a poem on Glashare Castle in that county. A daughter of his, Grania by name, was married to the owner of this castle, who was " pardoned ", too, in 1602. Tuileagna Mac Torna also wrote a poem in praise of Sir Nicholas Walshe, who was prominent as a judge in Ireland under Elizabeth.

This poet calls Lough Derg Eire's chief shrine and pilgrimage, chosen by Patrick as a place of penance. He repeats the assurance of the other bards that penance in the cave there is efficacious for sinners ; personally, it is his only hope. Humbly he says that he takes it as a " presage of mercy " that he had been enabled to make the pilgrimage at all, and he breaks out into a passionate access of affection for the lake, so quiet and grey, with its quality of other-worldliness and its soft-sounding shores, to him the lake of all lakes, a very Paradise. The authentic voice of the Irish people is expressed in an outburst of this kind. Mac Torna commends his soul to Patrick and begs salvation through him; he says that love for Lough Derg is certain to find the weak spot in the saint's heart! He asserts that penance such as one can do at Lough Derg is the only remedy for a stony heart, a hard eye and a deceitful mouth. This poet, too, came to Lough Derg in quest of contrition, but he was very dissatisfied with his measure of sorrow, wondering why he could weep so readily for worldly losses and then find himself without a tear for the wounded side and the pierced feet of Christ. He asks Our Lady to watch over his vigil in the cave and make it profitable for him. He acclaims Lough Derg as the road on which to follow the Creator, calling it " the guiding-star of East and West."

The Younger Feargal Mac Ward was another very interesting pilgrim bard who visited Lough Derg at the close of the sixteenth century. He was attached to the household of the military diplomat, Turlough Lynagh O'Neill. He wrote a poem in high praise of this chieftain's rule in which he cites the three famous evidences of good government : when a woman may journey alone, unchallenged, from Tory to Dundalk ; when nut-laden branches may overhang the roads and remain unplucked by lawless hands ; when a man can lose his cloak upon the highway and, returning for it afterwards, recover it. This poet wrote a charming little " Farewell to Lough Derg." Some modern Irish poet should seriously consider supplying an English verse-form for it, which an Irish composer might set to music, so that it could be sung by pilgrims leaving the island instead of the present " Farewell to Lough Derg " sung to-day, an unhappy example of doggerel and bathos. MacWard calls the island " shrine of men's salvation and chief pilgrimage of Eire." His sentiments are often expressed by pilgrims to-day, too : he is sorry to leave the " Beds," painful though he has found them ; even the solitary tree on

the island is saluted by him with a sigh. During his stay
here, his heart has been quite seized with love for the
" angel-haunted cave " so perfectly devised for curing
men of their stiff-necked pride.

A contemporary bard was Angus Mac Hugh Roe
O Higginn, who wrote on Lough Derg about the year
1590. He was another who had apparently resigned
himself to the inevitable, as he had been " pardoned "
with the anticipated sequel of a grant of land in Tirawley.
His poem is particularly interesting, as it was composed
during an actual pilgrimage before the all-night vigil.
Critics competent in the matter say that he had supreme
mastery of his craft. It is a curious picture to think of
him, probably at intervals between Stations, employing
his skill in metrical form to compose a poem on the
business of the moment. He is in a happy mood because
he found that the moment he landed on the island,
he achieved contrition : " I shed tears I had not thought
to shed . . . . My state of soul is now a cause of great joy to
me ; the greatest of all miracles has been wrought in myself." He expressed the positive belief, persistently held
by the Irish to the present day, that Patrick has a special
predilection for those who seek him in the Purgatory.
He asks the saint to stand by his side in the cave at the
opening of the long vigil, lest sleep should overpower
him. O'Higgin does not include among his prayers that
for a long life. He has original ideas on this subject :
" Man is forever speeding to the grave, whether he likes
it or not, even if all Adam's race were to try to save him
from it. Why should I ask for length of days ? The
Creator of the world got no long spell of life in it."

There is extant another poem by him on Lough Derg
in which he asserts that it is a privilege to be able to
make the pilgrimage and to look upon the cave where
Patrick dwelt. Through that powerful intercession,
an accumulation of sins is lifted from the soul. The
Passion of Christ is the great focus of contemplation on
the island and fear of the Last Judgment should be ever

present in the pilgrim's mind. But Patrick's protection
is a certainty. This poet is the first of the bards to in-
voke also the other saints commemorated in the penitential
" Beds " on Station Island : Columcille, Brendan,
Brigid, Molaise, Dabheoc and Catherine, " that holy
and humble maid." Forgiveness for sin is his chief
petition.

One would really imagine that the Irish bards had
never even heard of the fantasies ! Yet they must have
known about them. It is quite impossible to imagine
that no echo from that large *corpus* of European literature
had ever reached their ears ; or that they had never
even heard of those foreign notabilities travelling through
Ireland with their retinues. The Irish bards must have
known about the fantasies, but the fact is they did not
think the matter worth a single half-line of poetry, or
even the most cursory allusion. The hunger for visions
and facility in inventing them arose from a kind of
spirituality with which the bardic poets had absolutely
nothing in common : to them it smelt of morbidity
and disease ; their form of religion was so clean and hard
by comparison, they could entertain for the miracle-
mongers no sentiments save wonder, distaste, perhaps
resentment. Both the Irish poets and their less cultured
brethren went to the island in the mood of athletes
prepared to endure, with no hope of any reward, not
even sensible consolation. Even if contrition were
denied to them, their belief in the rite remained
unshaken. The native appraisement of the devotion
was the original idea ; it is that which has endured.
The other is like the crests of foam spouted to the surface
by the lake when it boils up in a sudden storm—that
afterwards vanish without trace.

Lough Derg and its islands and all the land surrounding
the lake, mainly comprised in the present parish of
Templecarne, went under the name of Termon-Dabheoc
down to the middle of the sixteenth century. After that

the Saint's name dropped out of the nomenclature and the estate was called Termon-Magrath after the Magraths, who were the hereditary chieftains of the district. Towards the close of the sixteenth century, Termon-Magrath was surrendered to Queen Elizabeth by Donough Magrath, who at that period held the title to the property. The surrender was compulsory, its purpose being to give the English rulers a title to the area. " Surrender and Re-grant " was the fiction by which they claimed to reorganize the country on more efficient lines. Property of this kind was legally surrendered, measured and estimated, and then re-granted at once to the original owner at a nominal rental. The scheme worked deviously in different parts of the country ; it does not concern us here. Many owners never got back their property at all on any terms. In the case of Termon-Magrath, it was understood that the territory was to be immediately re-granted to Donough Magrath for life and to his heirs subsequently. The bargain appears to have been kept in the main, so far as the Magrath family was concerned. But the matter was complicated by the fact that Donough Magrath was not the sole owner of Termon-Magrath ; the Church in this case also had legal rights to the property.

Surrender of the land that included the famous shrine had most adverse effects upon the Lough Derg pilgrimage. This devotion was henceforth handicapped with a legacy of trouble in the shape of disputed ownership of the site, an entirely new condition of affairs. For sixteen hundred years, whatever may have been its vicissitudes, its ownership by the Church had not been challenged. When the monastery had been established on Saints' Island for the guardianship of the Purgatory, a certain endowment had been allotted for its upkeep. The lands providing this revenue were later designated the parish of Templecarne, when the church parishes were outlined. Of course this parish did not belong exclusively to the religious community on Saints' Island. According to a precept recognised by the Brehon laws, land of this description was vested in two legatees : in the heir of the person who gave the original endowment, and in the successors of the original recipient of the property. Therefore, in the case of the division of land known as Termon-Magrath, its ownership was vested jointly in the Magrath family and in the ecclesiastical ruler of the parish.

Donough Magrath, then, was not legally entitled to make an unconditional surrender to Queen Elizabeth of the whole of Termon-Magrath. But by the date of that surrender the Catholic religion in Ireland was proscribed and, where Church property was concerned, a free-for-all policy was in force. The Reformation was well under way in England, where Catholics were violently suppressed. The same persecution was being waged in Ireland. The Magrath family became apostates. They conformed with the State religion for expediency. Donough, the head of the family, tried to make the title to the property safe for himself and for his sons.

The change in the legal ownership of Termon-Magrath meant, in practice, that Saint Patrick's Purgatory was thrown to the wolves. The next step in the legal procedure was a survey of the Magrath territory by the Elizabethan officers. As a result, that holy place, held for centuries as what we should call nowadays a national trust, was appended to the alien invaders. Misfortune, from this moment and for a very long period afterwards, engulfs the island history. Sworn enemies of race and creed would have been easier to deal with than when they were in combination with a ruthless Irish apostate.

Donough's eldest son was Miler Magrath, an intriguing, arresting, but disreputable personage. He had begun life as a Franciscan priest and was ordained in Rome, where he had completed most of his studies. He was then sent to Ireland to minister to his own people. In due time he was raised to the Catholic Bishopric of Down and Connor. He was acting as bishop for two years when he apostatized, but he still held on to the episcopal see. In 1570, he was made *Protestant* Bishop of Clogher. Some months later, he was promoted to the Protestant

Archbishopric of Cashel. All this while, he did not inform the Pope of his apostasy, but he took advantage of the times' confusion to continue to function—in a fashion of his own—as Catholic Bishop of Down and Connor, while holding the other two Protestant sees. In short, he was willing to collect from both churches everything that came his way in the matter of distinction and revenue.

It was 1580 before the Pope learned of Miler's behaviour, such was the state of communications. He then formally removed from office this extraordinary man who had pulled off the feat of combining for nine years the duties of Catholic Bishop and Protestant Archbishop.

Miler was a supreme cynic. He enjoyed high favour with Queen Elizabeth and made the best possible use of his luck. Even the crowd of Elizabethan land-grabbers and looters whom he had joined were shocked at his pluralities. He was probably the most notorious example in Ireland of this form of corruption. At the height of his career this new owner of Termon-Magrath battened on the revenues from one archbishopric, Cashel ; three bishoprics : Waterford, Lismore and Emly ; and no less than seventy parishes ! When complaints were made about him he squared his censors with a bribe and then laughed at them.

He was described as the most handsome man in Ireland. However, he cut a poor figure in the pulpit as he was no preacher. He was rather addicted to whiskey, but the habit seemed to prolong his life, as he lived to be 101. He was twice married after his apostasy : his first wife was and remained until her death a Catholic. He had a large family, numbering at least eight sons and one daughter, for all of whom he made handsome provision. Five of those sons are mentioned in the historic re-grant of Termon-Magrath by Queen Elizabeth to Miler's father, Donough.

It is affirmed in defence of Miler Magrath that he never swerved from his inner allegiance to Rome, and that e apostatized, as one should say nowadays, with a mental reservation. He had a habit of expressing concern about the state of his soul and of his own chances of salvation, which his Protestant brethren found exasperating. He would also discuss repentance and add that he hoped for death-bed reconciliation with Rome. In effect, he found it impossible to escape from the edict ' a priest forever '. Once, when acting as Protestant Archbishop of Cashel, he chanced to come upon a man lying by the roadside. Finding that he was a Catholic, Magrath prepared him for death according to the rites of the Catholic Church. He never took any part in the persecution of Catholics : in fact he secretly shielded them.

When Magrath's neighbour, Sir Brian O'Rourke, the rebel, was being led out to the scaffold at Tyburn, in 1591, Magrath, who happened to be present, offered his spiritual ministrations, which were scornfully rejected. At the end of it all, Magrath died reconciled to the Catholic Church. His name is still commemorated in the ruins of a castle that he built on the shore of Lough Erne.

The doom of the Augustinian monastery on Saints' Island was sealed long before the actual date of Donough Magrath's surrender. The Canons Regular of Saint Augustine must have been obliged to leave the island considerably before that event. At any rate, seven years after the date of the transfer, the Priory on Saints' Island is described in an Ulster Requisition taken in Donegal as "much in decay and for many years past totally abandoned and dissolved."

At first, however, the suppression of Lough Derg was motived more by material greed than by religious fanaticism. The aggressor was satisfied when he had seized the monastic property. Although the walls of the buildings on Saints' Island had been levelled in token of the monks' dispossession, the pilgrimage went on. In documents dated about 1600, reference is made to a Canon being in charge of the ceremonies there. He either accompanied the pilgrims, or he took up temporary residence on Station Island for the pilgrimage season.

During those years the pilgrimage was frequented by
both laymen and priests, the latter including the Archbishop of Tuam. The vigil was carried out in the narrow
cave by fourteen men at a time. One assumes that when
the spurious cave on Saints' Island was filled in by order
of the Pope in 1497, the original cave on Station Island
was left untouched and its use was afterwards resumed.
An Irish script by Michael O'Clery, preserved in the
Brussels Royal Library and translated by Father
Grosjean, S.J., describes the Lough Derg " Station," or
round of penance, as it was then performed. The tentative
date of 1600 has been assigned to Michael O'Clery's
script.

It is interesting, and the modern pilgrim will probably
find it a moving study, to compare this document of
the early seventeenth century with the leaflet used by
pilgrims on the island at the present day. The points of
similarity are striking and stamp the devotion as an
extraordinary instance of continuity. The order of
making the " Station " is unchanged, as the pilgrim
then began, as now, at the Church, moved from that
to the " Beds," then to the water's edge, and so the
Church again. The total number of Paters, Aves and
Creeds recited on this round of penance is practically
the same to-day as it was in 1600, so jealously has the
traditional rite been preserved :—

> " It is thus the Round of Lough Derg which is
> called the Purgatory of Patrick should be performed,
> according to the instructions of the wise men of the
> Purgatory.
> " First when beginning the Round, after entering
> the Chapel or Church, to kneel, to recite *Pater*, *Ave
> Maria* and *Credo*, and to give a kiss to the Church
> door when going out, keeping the Church to thy
> right westwards and to give a kiss to the old Cross
> which is in front of the Church and keeping the
> Cross to thy right, northwards to the side of the
> Church and to give a kiss to the stone, which is

at the side of the Church, and to go northwards
hence to the Cross and to the Cairn, which are on
the eastern side of the Church and to give a kiss to
the stone which is on the northern side in the Cairn,
and to take to the right on the other side of the
Cairn . . . . and to go seven times round the Church
. . . . And when the seventh time is performed,
go to the Cross which is on the western side of the
Church, as we have said, and give it a kiss and
northward again to the other stone which is at the
side of the Church, and give a kiss and go from the
north again, retracing thy steps, between the Church
and the old Cross we have mentioned, and go west-
wards directly from the Cross to Brendan's Bed
and give a kiss to a certain stone, which is in the
door of the bed, and go three times righthand wise
round the Bed, reciting certain prayers, on the
outside, and go three more times in the same way
inside and say three *Paters*, three *Ave Maria* and
Credo on thy knees . . . . to Brigid's Bed, and do the
same thing . . . . to Catherine's Bed, and do the
same thing . . . . to Colum Cille's Bed and do the
same thing. And after completing thy prayers there,
keeping the same bed to thy right hand and northwards around it to Patrick's Bed and give a kiss
to the uneven stone which is near the door of the
Cave. The two Beds of Dabheoc and Molaise form
one bed that is knit and joined together with Patrick's
bed. And go seven times round them all, etc."

Certain differences between the instructions issued to
pilgrims at that time and those followed to-day have of
course been made necessary by the vicissitudes of its
history. Even though the fury of the Danes had done
its worst to the place in the ninth century, there were
far more relics preserved in 1600 than now, including
carved stones and a bell of St. Patrick broken into three
fragments. In addition, there were certain holy stones
in the lake revered for their reputed direct association

with Patrick. All such memorials, which have now disappeared forever, were venerated by the seventeenth-century pilgrim on his rounds. There was, too, a " Bed ' dedicated to St. Patrick, which was peculiarly situated : it lay outside but joined on to the double " Bed ' dedicated to Saints Molaise and Dabheoc, and was entered only through the latter. It appears probable that pilgrims did not enter St. Patrick's Bed ; they only prayed at the entrance to it.

The Royal Irish Academy collection includes no less than seven eighteenth-century manuscripts giving a metrical " Instructions to Pilgrims." This is a very interesting poem because it records in convenient verse-form that which Michael O'Clery has given in prose. The poem begins : *A dhuine theid go Loch Dearg* (" The Pilgrimage of Lough Derg according to the Psalter of Cashel "). Between the pilgrimage as it is thus described and the pilgrimage as it is made to-day, there are the same slight differences as remarked in O'Clery's script : for example, one begins at Brendan's Bed instead of Brigid's ; and the two Beds described to-day as the " large peni-tential Bed " are described as " Patrick's Bed and Saint Molaise's side by side in one doorway, that makes six ; And the seventh Dabheoc's, who was greatly loved." It is clear from Michael O'Clery's script, that fragment quoted from the Psalter of Cashel, and the allusions in the poem by Angus Mac Hugh Roe O Higginn that the Lough Derg pilgrimage rite has remained practically unchanged for nearly four hundred years.

The pilgrimage was of course incomparably harder three hundred years ago than it is to-day. It lasted nine days instead of three, during which the pilgrim's fast was broken once a day with bread and water instead of the more stimulating bread and tea now permitted. The vigil in the cave lasted twenty-four hours, instead of the modern all-night watch in the Church. The vigil in those days was accompanied by a severe intensi-fication of the fast for three days, no food whatever being taken the day before the vigil or while in the cave or during the succeeding day. Finally, on emerging from the cave, the pilgrim plunged three times under the lake water as a symbol of his cleansing. Until about the year 1560 the pilgrimage had always lasted fifteen days. Many pilgrims of the 1600 era must have deplored the mitigation of the rite, for they continued to make a pilgrimage lasting fifteen days.

When the shrine was taken from the Church, rightful joint owners of lake and island, the fact at first made little apparent difference to the main body of pilgrims, the Irish people, who looked upon the sanctuary as their special possession. Even when the Augustinians were driven out and the place left without protectors, the yearly tide of pilgrims did not diminish. The expulsion of the monks was considered a temporary blow from which the holy island would recover. No-one attachèd the idea of permanence to that misfortune. It was this fortitude, this inability to see defeat, which carried the pilgrimage through the succeeding century, the darkest in its history.

VI. SUPPRESSION

THE seventeenth century is a painful passage in Irish history. The detailed story of the Lough Derg pilgrimage during this period is only a reflection of the total Irish defeat.

The Flight of the Earls early in the century had left in the country only defenceless non-combatants upon whom the conqueror forced the reformed religion. Roman Catholic priests were banished by proclamation. At this time the ruling power was bigoted to a fanatical degree, and was resolved to destroy every Catholic shrine and memorial in the country. It was inevitable that the island in Lough Derg should be blacklisted. St. Patrick's Purgatory had already suffered when greed was the motive for plundering the sanctuary. That picture of the Augustinian Priory on Saints' Island as " for many years past totally abandoned and dissolved " describes it. But mere abandonment and decay would not satisfy bigotry, which knew no appeasement until the very stones of the sanctuary were broken up into rubble and scattered.

It is here the Franciscans enter, with great glory to themselves, into the history of Lough Derg. The place had become such a target of the persecutors that no cloistered order of religious could any longer be its custodians. But who would undertake the charge? Priests had to be found courageous enough to endure the hardships of the place and give the Sacraments to the crowds of pilgrims still flocking to the island. There is a letter in the archives of the Franciscan Abbey, Merchants' Quay, Dublin, dated 11th March, 1631, addressed to Rome by the then Primate of Ireland, Hugh O'Reilly, begging that the Purgatory should be given into the official charge of the Franciscans. He states that the reason for his choice of the friars for this uninviting work is because they are " the best suited to rough places." In all Franciscan literature I do not know more appropriate praise. But those men who had chosen the " rough places " not merely of this world, but of the inner life too, had in fact already come to the rescue at the time that letter was written. The Irish Primate merely wished to get Rome's approbation to a move that had already been made. He pointed out in the letter that in this transfer of guardianship there had been no conflict with the Canons Regular of St. Augustine who, on account of their sadly reduced numbers and the impossibility of living according to their rule among the roofless ruins on Saints' Island, were very willing—for the time being at least—to give up their charge.

We have this picture, then, from authentic documents, of crowds of pilgrims flocking to the holy island during the summer of 1631 and among them the Franciscans, who looked after these people " with their customary fervour of soul and alacrity of spirit . . . . particularly prepared to sustain the weight and burden of the day," in the words of Archbishop Hugh O'Reilly.

The Franciscans were running great danger. The Government had already particularly condemned the Order of Friars and a special proclamation had long since been issued for their suppression. On St. Stephen's Day, 1629, the Protestant Archbishop Bulkeley, at the head of a troop of soldiers, had forcibly entered the Franciscan Church in Dublin and had had all the friars there arrested. Under his supervision the soldiers desecrated the altar and broke up the statue of St. Francis. This was typical of the fury with which the Catholic religion was being attacked everywhere in Ireland about the same time.

The year 1632 was ebb-tide in the history of Lough Derg. The Government became fatally interested in it and their determination to destroy it shows the popularity of the pilgrimage and its high place in Irish life. It was considered such a rallying-point of devotion and loyalty

F

that it would simply have to be extinguished if the Catholic religion were ever to be stamped out.

The first move was made when the Earl of Cork and the Lord Chancellor sent " persons of quality " to make all enquiries about the ridiculous business of the Purgatory and report to them. As was only to be expected, the report was very contemptuous ; the claims of Lough Derg were exaggerated and misrepresented in order that scorn could be poured on them. The enquirers—

"found that this miraculous cave descending down to the bottom of hell was no other than a little cell digged out of the rock without any window or holes, so as the door being shut, it was utterly dark, being of so little depth that a tall man could not stand upright in it, and of no greater capacity than to hold six or seven persons . . . . The Lords Justices caused the Fryers to depart and laid the whole open and exposed to the air."

Those persons of quality who had visited the Purgatory on the instructions of the Earl of Cork and the Lord Chancellor had certainly made a gesture to discourage the pilgrimage, but they had not done enough.

Subsequent reports received must have been unsatisfactory because the Government now made a second and a better attempt to end the pilgrimage, the details of which are given in a letter from a certain Sir William Stuart to the Privy Council. It appears that Lord Balfour directed Sir William and a number of others to meet on a given day at the shore of the lake for the purpose of " seizing unto his Majesty's use St. Patrick's Purgatory." Stuart, like an obedient servant, repaired to the meeting-place on the appointed day in June, but no-one else came. He reports that he waited about " in the comfortless place almost two days and one night, none coming." It would look as though those gentlemen of quality found their orders distasteful ; anyhow they showed an understandable dislike for the wild shores of the lake and its tumultuous waters, a scene desolate enough even on a June day.

Sir William appears to have done nothing at first but moon about uncertainly with his company of horsemen, whom he probably entertained with picturesque comments. He goes on to say that he then got certain information about the island :—

> "the Abbot, Priests and Friers which were in the island had gotten knowledge of your Lordship's directions : whereupon in the night time they stole out of the Island in a boat, which at the least would carry forty persons."

The Friars had already been formally expelled from the island. This time they apparently judged it better to leave before they were driven out.

Finally, when nobody else turned up at the lake shore Sir William apparently decided to take action on his own account. He commandeered the only boat available and crossed over to the island, where he found four hundred and thirty-one people making the pilgrimage. This was a surprising number, in the face of the discouragement the pilgrimage was then having. Stuart took charge on the island and rounded up the pilgrims, shipping them back in companies to the mainland "without any kind of violence," he is careful to explain. He then returned the boat to Master James Magrath, its owner (son of Miler Magrath), with suitable cautions that the island was to be no longer frequented on any pretext, by Order of the Privy Council.

The next move was an Order directed to Master James Magrath, owner of the island, under the signatures of the Earl of Cork and the Lord Chancellor, requiring that he—

> "should enter into a bond to the Clerk of the Council, to his Majesty's use of one thousand pounds sterling to pull down and utterly demolish that monster of fame called St. Patrick's Purgatory with St. Patrick's Bed and all the vaults, cells and other houses and buildings : and to have all the other superstitious stones and materials cast into the Lough and that he should suffer the superstitious

Chapel in the Island to be pulled down to the
ground and no boat to be there nor pilgrimage
used nor frequented during James Magrath's
life willingly, or wittingly."

James Magrath had already been cautioned by Sir
William Stuart that the island of St. Patrick's Purgatory
was to be considered " seized unto his Majesty's use "
and that he, Magrath, was not to allow the traffic of
pilgrims to and fro.

One judges from this increase of pressure that Magrath
must have been reluctant in obeying orders.   Probably
revenue (certainly not friendship for the pilgrimage)
is the explanation.   After all, the island was his,
since Termon-Magrath had been " re-granted " to his
family in 1610 for ten pounds a year. Magrath must have
been deriving some income from his ferry rights, which
were estimated to be worth over £200 a year during the
following century.   His family had given up the Faith
for the sake of their property ; were they now to see
their property, too, taken from them ?

Magrath did not carry out the destruction on Saints'
Island that he had been ordered to supervise. The threat
was carried out and the next thing that happened was
that he was taken into custody by the Sergeant-at-Arms,
under bond of £1,000.   Son of a man who had been so
highly favoured at court and member of such a notable
family of apostates, it was a foregone conclusion that
Magrath would extricate himself from this difficulty.
He must have been fertile in excuses, of which the most
plausible probably was that he could get no labourer
to do the work of destruction for him.   When, later, his
masters took the job in hand themselves they found it
an insuperable difficulty to get local men to do it. Finally
they had to resort to the imported servants of planters,
as no natives could be either bribed or coerced into
levelling St. Patrick's Purgatory.

With Magrath in custody, the Government issued a
new order specifically naming those who were to see

that the work of destruction was carried out on the island :—

The Order of the Lords Justices and Council Anent Lough Derg and James Magrath. 1632.

" Forasmuch as the frequent and public resort of people in great numbers to that place or Island called St. Patrick's Purgatory, there performing superstitions, ceremonies, pilgrimages and offerings, is so extremely abusive and superstitious as is not fit to be endured. We therefore taking the same unto our due consideration and foreseeing that albeit there may be a cessation there for a time from those abuses and superstitions in regard they observe the State to resent the same : Yet many times the seduced people will secretly find opportunity to resort hither and so by stealths continue their superstitious abuses, while the place standeth as now it does. We have therefore adjudged it the best and fittest means to prevent and wholly take away the continuance of that abuse hereafter, that the place be defaced and utterly demolished. And therefore we do hereby order and resolve that Letters shall be dispatched from this board unto the Rev. Father in God the Lord Bishop of Clogher, Sir John Dundarre High Sheriff of the County of Donegal, Edward Archdale and Leonard Blennerhasset esq. and Archbald Areskon Clerk or any three or more of them, whereof the said Lord Bishop or Sir John Dunbarre or Edward Tarleton to be always one. Requiring and authorizing them or any three or more of them as aforesaid : by or before the third day of Dec. next to cause the Chapel and all the Irish houses now situate in that Island called St Patrick's Purgatory, all the buildings, pavements, walls, works, foundations, Circles, Caves, Cells and Vaults thereof of lime or stone or otherwise to be broken down, defaced and utterly demolished, and that also called St. Patrick's Bed, as also that rock or stone standing in the water there having a clift in it, which (as is vainly said) St. Patrick made kneeling at his prayers : And also that stone covered there with water, which hath the point of a man's foot and which (as the seduced people do believe) St. Patrick made with standing thereupon and likewise all other things there, whereunto those superstitious people have used to go in Pilgrimage : and that they cause all the stones to be thrown into the Lough or water wherein the Island standeth, saving only such of the stones of the said Chapel as James Magrath the proprietor of the land will forthwith carry clear out of the Island and make use of in some other place. We do also order that the same James Magrath shall forthwith enter into bond to the Clerk of the Council for His Majesty's use the sum of one thousand pounds English with the condition to bear all the charges necessary for the performing of all that by this order is required to be done and not to suffer any interruption or impediment to be given thereunto. And that such of the stones of the Chapel as the said James shall carry out, shall not at any time hereafter during his life with his permission be again returned to that Island. And that he shall from time to time take order that no person or persons be at any time admitted during his life with his permission or knowledge or privily to go into that place or Island called St. Patrick's Purgatory, to the end to say Mass there or to perform any Pilgrimage, offerings or any other superstitious ceremonies there. And that he shall suffer no Boat to be kept there to pass to and from the said Island. And that during his life there shall not be any conventions there of Jesuits, Friars, priests, Nuns or any other superstitious Orders of the Popish pretended Clergy, that the said Magrath shall be able to prevent, which Bond being so entered into, the Sergeant-at-Arms, in whose custody the said Magrath now remaineth, is upon certificate hereof from the

Clerk of the Council to release the said Magrath,
he paying his due fees."

The personages named in the Order were not of course
expected to execute it with their own hands, but only
diligently to supervise it. To demolish even such a
humble group of buildings as were then found on Station
Island and scatter the stones in the water was, however,
a considerable task. Willing labourers were needed and
implements such as crowbars, picks and battering-
rams, a boat or boats, at least a day's provisions for the
expedition and, finally, experienced boatmen to row
over, because the passage from shore to island includes
some dangerous rocks, requiring a knowledgeable pilot.

Among the five gentlemen named in the Order of the
Lords Justices, one alone showed any enthusiasm or
diligence in carrying out instructions : he was " the
Reverend Father in God the Lord Bishop of Clogher,"
Spottiswoode. He left a written account of his work,
from which we learn that, when he first received the
Council's Order, he immediately called on his superior,
the Protestant Archbishop of Armagh to find out that
prelate's views. His Archbishop gave him every encouragement to obey the Order to the letter. We gather
that the two Protestant ecclesiastics settled down to a
long discussion of St. Patrick's Purgatory. (Their conclusions, incidentally, are high praise of the devotion.)
The Archbishop had rightly come to the conclusion
that the cave was the whole focus of interest there.
He told his subordinate to make certain of *that*, whatever
happened, and to get rid of it completely. Spottiswoode
was to make a thorough examination of the whole site,
make absolutely certain that he had the right cave, and
then have it dug up to the very foundations, scattered
and filled in. He was literally not to leave a stone un-
turned so as to disperse once and for all the atmosphere
of awe and mystery so persistently clinging to the place.

Fortified with priestly encouragement, Spottiswoode got
to work next day. He sent a copy of the Council's Order

to each of his fellow-Commissioners named in it, appointing them to meet him " at the town next Lough Derg " on the 25th of October. The answers he received were disappointing. There was no enthusiasm. The others dwelt on the difficulty of the order. They said one hundred men could hardly complete it in a fortnight. They said they were perfectly willing themselves to meet his Lordship at the place and on the date appointed, but if they did so, they would be coming alone, for they could get " none to accompany them, or any labourer or tools upon any terms."

How eloquently that silent, depopulated and defeated countryside could still express itself ! The people of Donegal were starving and impoverished, but no bribe could induce any of them to take part in the destruction of St. Patrick's Purgatory ; for such a task, there was neither a labourer nor a tool in the whole county.

Spottiswoode, however, was not deterred. He wrote back to the recalcitrant Commissioners named in the Order, again insisting that they should meet him as arranged, and that he himself would bring the necessary workmen and tools. He was as good as his word. He him-self reached Lough Derg on the evening before the day appointed, bringing with him " Some twenty able men . . . . well armed . . . . with all sorts of tools fitting for the service."

In his subsequent report to his Archbishop, he pointed out that, but for his forethought, nothing would have been done. The High Sheriff of Donegal failed to turn up. Another of his fellow-Commissioners brought only one serving-man with him and, moreover, seemed out of temper and disgruntled with the whole affair, and refused to cross over to the island. Everything conspired to discourage Spottiswoode. When he left the comparative shelter and warmth of the " town next Lough Derg," it was raining hard. He had to wait on the bleak shore of the lake " without any shelter to horse or man " three hours before the boat could be found. Then the wind rose ominously and white horses capped the water. Having

at last secured the boat, the bishop could get no-one to
steer it through the rocks. Everyone he spoke to tried
to put him off. He was warned that his food supplies
might run short, because in stormy seasons the lake
was sometimes not navigable for as long as ten days
or a fortnight at a time.

But this Spottiswoode was a fanatical champion of
reformed religion. The whispers of the country people
that Saint Patrick would bring some dire misfortune on
himself and his company made him only the more determined. He finally got his men on to the island and they
set to work. His report to the Archbishop goes on to
say :—

> " The first thing I searched diligently after was
> the Cave, wherein I remembered your Grace
> enjoined me to dig to the very foundations and leave
> no corner unsought and so I did ; I caused to dig
> about it on all sides till I came to the rock but
> found no appearance of any secret passage either
> to the Chapel or to the Lough : neither would the
> nature of the ground suffer it, in a word this cave
> was a poor beggarly hole, made with some stones,
> laid together with men's hands without any great
> art : and after covered with earth such as husband-
> men make to keep a few hogs from the rain. When
> I could find nothing there, I undermined the
> Chapel, which was well covered with shingles and
> brought all down together. Then we brake down
> the Circles and Saints' beds which were like so
> many coalpits and so pulled down some great
> Irish houses. Thus when I had defaced all saving
> one Irish house : I came out of the Island myself
> and left one half of my men behind to pull that down
> also so soon as they should see me landed not sooner ;
> lest if by a storm we were driven back, we might
> want a place to shelter us. The country people
> expected that St. Patrick would have wrought
> some miracle but thanks be to God none of my
> Company received any other harm but the bad

ways, broken cawsies and the dangerous going in a
little boat : yet our comfort is, we effected that
for which we came hither, which was more than
we expected could be done in so short a time,
which hath wonderfully displeased them that were
bewitched with these fooleries. But that I do
not much stand upon, in regard I have also obeyed
the command of the State and punctually also
done what your Grace did enjoin, etc.,

> *James Clogher.*"

For the second time in one year St. Patrick's cave
had been attacked with pick and crowbar. Spottiswoode
left the little island, which is less than an acre in extent,
entirely covered with scattered stones and rubble. Every
cherished memorial had been broken up and defaced.
When a modern pilgrim complains of the absence of
Patrician and mediaeval relics from a site so long
venerated, the answer is 1632. On that wild October
day, insofar as man could encompass it, the place had
been destroyed. Spottiswoode returned from that
expedition convinced that Saint Patrick's Purgatory
was finished, " utterly demolished," effaced forever. It
was all over. Nothing was left.

A close watch was then kept for some years and no-
one was allowed access to the island. And yet the
pilgrimage went on ! The people assembled on the lake
shores and went through the whole ritual, just as they
used to do on the island, including the fast and vigil,
often pausing in their prayers—it is said—to extend
their arms to the holy island to which they were denied
entrance. The moment vigilance was relaxed the people
began to drift back ! Anyone who knows Lough Derg
will see the joke of trying to police it. When the south-
western approach to the island was patrolled, they
would make the longer journey to it from the north-
east. When the boat was taken away, they built another
boat. Moreover, the people knew the lie of the land and
the lake, which the despoilers did not.

James Magrath extricated himself from his troubles
with the Privy Council. But Termon-Magrath, enshrining
that island of obloquy, had become a thorny possession.
He would have been glad to be rid of it. After an interval,
he succeeded in making over his lease to none other than
the man who had razed the sanctuary, James Spottiswoode himself, Protestant Bishop of Clogher. Considering
the times, Magrath probably thought he was lucky to
get anything out of that property. It was the curious
fate of St. Patrick's Purgatory thus to become included
in the see lands of the Irish Protestant Church !
Thenceforward James Magrath probably had peace.
And Protestantism did its very utmost to stamp out
every vestige of the pilgrimage and make its resurgence
in the future an impossible hope.

The personnel of the English Government in Ireland
happened to be changed during the six years following
the action taken by Spottiswoode. We then find Queen
Henrietta Maria, consort of Charles I, making an appeal
(which was written in her own hand) to the Irish Viceroy,
Lord Wentworth, on behalf of the Irish people, asking
that they should be allowed to continue their pilgrimage
to St. Patrick's Purgatory. She wrote in queenly style
as follows :—

" Monsieur Wentworth,
    I have written to you before for requests ; in
which I have recognized you were so prompt to
oblige me that I was compelled to write to you
myself to give you my thanks ; and also to beg
you one thing, which is that you would not be
willing to allow a devotion, which the people of
this country have always had at a certain place to
St. Patrick, to be abolished. They will avail themselves of it so modestly that you will have no reason
to regret it ; and you would do me a great pleasure.
I am giving Monsieur Antrim charge to entreat

the matter with you. For this reason I shall finish in assuring you that you will not find me ungrateful but one who will make apparent on every occasion the desire she has to oblige you and who will always be your very good friend."

Although she had signed herself *Votre bien bonne amie*, the Queen received a refusal from Lord Wentworth. His letter is nearly a perfect model of a polite refusal :—

" Dublin Castle, Oct. 10, 1638.

" May it please your most excellent Majesty—

The gracious lines I received in your Majesty's own hand concerning St. Patrick's Purgatory I shall convey over to my posterity as one of the greatest honours of my past life. For the thing itself, it was by Act of State decryed under the government of the late Lords Justices, before my coming into this Kingdom, and since I read your Majesty's letter I can in truth say I am glad that none of my council was in the matter. Yet being now absolutely taken away, there will be greater difficulty to restore it than would be barely to continue and tolerate such a devotion prohibited by a smaller power or discontinued for a shorter time than this hath been. Besides the place is in the midst of the great Scottish Plantations ; and I fear at this time where some men's zeal hath run them already, not only beyond their wits, but almost forth of their allegiance too, it might furnish them of something to say in prejudice and in scandal at his Majesty's Government ; which for the present indeed is by all means to be avoided. Yet considering we often observe, that may be had in due season with ease which mistimed may prove unsafe and very difficult to obtain ; my most humble opinion is your Majesty may do passing wisely to let this devotion rest awhile, till there may be a fitter opportunity apprehended, by which to effect your

Majesty's satisfaction therein; which gracious
temper and forbearance shall also (in my judgment)
dispose and bow all nearer your Majesty's desires
than any other way that can for the present be
taken. And I beseech your Majesty to honour me
with this belief, that my duties in fulfilling your
commands are so broad awake, that in all or any,
where I may have the happiness or ability to
serve to your Majesty's contentment, I shall not
need the solicitation of my Lord of Antrim or any
other whatsoever to invite me thereunto; there
being nothing abroad which can put me so fast and
diligently on as my own great cheerfulness at home;
which unminded by any, shall through all your
gracious appointments, express me with all Faith
and attention."

Whom did Wentworth mean when he hinted at certain
powers " in the midst of the great Scottish Plantations
. . . . where some men's zeal hath run them already,
not only beyond their wits, but almost forth of their
allegiance too . . . . " ? Were those powers in the Irish
Protestant Church already so strongly entrenched that
even the Government could not touch them ?

The Papal Nuncio, Rinnucinni, accredited to the
Irish Confederation, was greatly attracted to Lough
Derg and its pitiful story. Before he was long in the
country he ambitioned in 1648 recovering this sanctuary
for the people. The plan to rescue the holy island
formed part of an expedition captained by the great
O'Neill. The proposal was as follows :—

" That they should recover Sligo situated on the
sea and on the confines and therefore very valuable
to Connaught. From this place they could pass
into Ulster and, attempting the strong castle of
Enniskillen, free from the hands of the heretics the
so much celebrated Purgatory of St Patrick. As

prayers have been offered up in this deep cave from
time immemorial so the date of their commence
ment is uncertain. It is known that the Saint chose
this place for his devotions in retirement and the
revelations which it pleased God to communicate
to him have been believed and perhaps proved by
posterity. At present the Calvinists in their rage
by levelling the ground have filled up the cavity
and as one can scarce discover any vestiges of the
place, so they endeavour to extinguish also the
memory of the fact. It appeared to me that this
equalled any of the most glorious of Apostolic
missions and that I should have in some measure
fulfilled my career, if in this place covered as much
by the insults as by the earth thrown on it by the
Puritans it had been granted to me again to plant
there the Cross. But I was not worthy of seeing
this hope carried into execution, the want and
tardy supply of money entirely ruined the design.'

St. Patrick's Purgatory had been officially abolished
and blotted out of memory. Neither the Queen of
England nor a Papal Nuncio could restore the shrine.
What is our surprise, therefore, to find it later, in 1701,
being made the subject of an Act of Queen Anne :—

> " And whereas the superstitions of Popery are greatly
> increased and upheld by the pretended sanctity of
> Places especially a place called St. Patrick's
> Purgatory in the County of Donegal . . . . "

By this time a whole century has passed, one hundred
years, since the Canons Regular of St. Augustine had
been expelled from their monastery on Saints' Island.
Even the children of the men who saw those calamities
take place must have passed away by this time and still
St. Patrick's Purgatory, only a little rocky island covered
with melancholy ruins, exerts on the people an influence
that can disquiet the State. It is obvious that what
neither a crowned head nor an accredited envoy from

the Pope could do, the people themselves had done—
they had restored the pilgrimage. After one hundred
years of repression, this is really an amazing state of
affairs.

The Statute goes on to prohibit assembly at Lough
Derg under penalty of a fine of ten shillings, in default of
which payment the offender was to be publicly whipped.
Now this punishment, it was confidently believed, would
surely put an end to the practice of assembly on that
island and on the lake shore.

About this time, a notable personage in the Irish
Protestant Church, the Archdeacon of Armagh, visited
the island through motives of curiosity, and wrote a
careful description of what he saw. Evidently pilgrims
had secretly done the very thing the Lords Justices had
so earnestly tried to safeguard against : they had been
as busy as ants with the stones, assuaging their grief
by collecting, sorting out and piling together again those
stones in an effort to identify and preserve the poor
island memorials. The pilgrimage was then being performed amidst mournful heaps of stones. The following
extract describes what Archdeacon Hewson saw :—

> " Having heard much talk of this place I went in
> company of other Protestants to visit and found as
> follows
>
> " The Lough situate in the Parish of Templecarn,
> Barony of Tirhugh and County of Donegal, is about
> three miles broad one way and two another : 'tis
> of no regular form, has in it one Peninsula and
> several small Islands.
>
> " The most famous (though not largest) of
> which lies on the South-East side of the Lough
> within less than a mile of the mainland : and is
> called St. Patrick's Purgatory : 'tis a barren
> rocky piece of ground, about eighty paces long
> and twenty broad except in the end next the shore
> where 'tis about thirty. In it these things and places
> are remarkable :

I. Towards the right hand of the landing place
a small heap of stones with a shank of a
Cross in it, which they call St. Patrick's
Altar.

II. Three or four paces beyond this another
small heap with a stone Cross placed on it

III. And a little beyond that a long heap o.
rubbish which is called St. Patrick's Cove

IV. Towards the left hand of the landing-place
are the ruins of a house and Chapel, which
were demolished by order of the Government
about the year 1680. In the Chapel ruins
are two poor Altars and near them two other
Coves.

V. Some paces beyond these are the Saints
Beds being six circles of stone : four of them
put carelessly together above a foot high
and five or six in diameter with a gap or
one side of each : and the floors rocky and
uneven. They stand in no order within two
or three paces of each other : the last two
Beds have their walls better made and some
what higher and one of them twice as large
as any of the rest. They bear the names o
Brenan, Bride, Catherine, Colum, Patrick and
Molossa in the largest Bed, and Avioge.

VI. In the farther end of the Island is a coarse
Altar erected to St. Patrick not many
years ago.

VII. Some few small trees and a large one half
withered are about the ruins and fifty small
huts in the nearer end of the Island for the
reception of pilgrims.

VIII. On the North-East side of which are three
lumps of rock, three or four paces within
the Lough almost continuous and a little
further in it the shank of a stone Cross al
about two foot above water."

Hewson's mention of " the ruins of a house and Chapel, which were demolished by order of the Government about the year 1680 " raises a problem. Is it possible to believe that any rebuilding took place on the island between the years 1632 and 1680 ? I think not. Nothing was left after the demolition of 1632. Seeing that the pilgrimage was so strictly prohibited, and the prohibition rigidly enforced for at least ten years after that, and that the rite was then only furtively and secretly resumed, it is difficult to believe that any building could have taken place on the island. Obviously Hewson meant to refer to the demolition order of 1632.

His account shows that not even a carved stone or a piece of wood had been left intact. Access to the Island had been forbidden by Act of Parliament under the severest penalties. A boat was not even allowed to be kept on the mainland for the purpose of getting across to it. The shores of the lake were watched to make certain that there was no assembly there. Lord Wentworth had described the pilgrimage to Queen Henrietta as " absolutely taken away." What more could have been done to make perfect the accuracy of that description ?

VII. THE PENAL NIGHT

THE work of the crowbar brigade in the destruction
of St. Patrick's Purgatory finds a certain reflection
in literature. It is rather like when a dead felon is
buried in quicklime as a final mark of contempt. When
the site of the pilgrimage was destroyed, a corrosive
accumulation of derision and ridicule was then heaped
upon it. Such a large group of writers used their abilities
in deriding Lough Derg they almost deserve to be called
a school, especially as much of their work gained considerable currency and was spread over a period of nearly
two hundred years. This outpouring of pens was a sort
of aftermath of the physical destruction and a mani-
festation of the persecution. Even apart from the object
on which its odium was fastened, this is a *corpus* of
writing worth a glance as a literary curiosity. It included such names as Henry Jones (1647), Hewson (1701),
Richardson (1727), Skelton (1786), Carleton (1813),
Lanigan (1822), Otway (1829), Inglis (1834), Hardy
(1836), and Wright (1844).

There were two methods of approach in holding up
to derision that which the writers considered a foolish,
or a dead, devotion : one was to attack the " fantasies "
as though belief in them were an article of faith ; the
other was to deride minor abuses, or ignorant and foolish
types of peasants, who turned up among the pilgrims, as
indeed they turn up in all places where crowds gather.
Even the most bitter enemies of the pilgrimage could say
little against the prayer, fasting and vigil that formed
the main part of it.

Bishop James Spottiswoode, whom we know, was
succeeded in the See of Clogher by a certain Henry Jones,
who wrote a book on St. Patrick's Purgatory mainly
railing against the " miraculous reports " with which it
was credited and the " superstitious practices " carried

on there. He says that even the very trees on the little
island had a miraculous origin : " Neither must it be
imagined, there being so few of them and they in so
holy a place, they would be there without a miracle."
There is reason to believe that this book was really
written by Spottiswoode, or that Jones compiled it from
the notes left by Spottiswoode. It seems curious to find
that when Spottiswoode had so satisfactorily blotted out
the shrine, he should have troubled to write so many
notes about it. It is very probable that, though it was
over and done with, he could not quite dismiss it from
his mind, and that the Notes he left represent his efforts
to get rid of a preoccupation he could not admit as
disturbing.

The Reverend John Richardson gave prominence to
Lough Derg in a book he wrote on *The Great Folly,
Superstition and Idolatry of Pilgrimages in Ireland* which
appeared in 1727. The title gives an indication of the
trend of the book. According to this author the priests
simply ran the place for profit and in order to work upon
the people's imagination. The account of St. Patrick's
Purgatory written by Archdeacon Hewson of Armagh
was published as an addition to Richardson's book.
If one disregards the misrepresentation in these writings,
they give some incidental information that is valuable.
Hewson gives a careful description of Station Island as
it was in 1701, quoted in the last chapter. Richardson
tells the story of a Breton pilgrim's attempts at excavation which is a very interesting page of history. If the
story of these excavations be true, this pilgrim from
Brittany must have been very inaccurately informed :—

> " In this Lake there are many Islands, the
> biggest of which is by some called St. Aveog's, who
> is said to have been buried in it : by others St.
> Fintanus and by others the Island of Saints. It
> is said that the passage into Purgatory was first
> found in this Island : but it being near the shore
> and a bridge from the mainland into it, which gave
> the people free and ready access, this passage into

Purgatory was stopped up and another opened in a less Island about half a mile away from the shore, by which means the Monks wisely gained two points, viz. the profit of a ferry boat for wafting the Pilgrims over the Lake and an opportunity of working further upon the imaginations of the people and making them believe that they were really going into another world. It is now said that this passage is hid from them for unknown reasons, but that in due time it will be discovered by some devout Pilgrim. This probably induced one, Ludovicus Pyrrhus, a native of Bretagne in France, to try if he could find it out. In order to this about 34 years ago (1693) he came to Lough Derg and employed labourers to dig and search for it throughout both these Islands, the neighbouring priests giving their assistance. He continued two summers at this work and after he had spent almost all the money he brought with him, fell a-trafficking and applied the profit to the same use. At last as he was searching among the rubbish of a dwelling house in the largest Island, he found a window with iron stanchers, Mr. Art MacCullen, Popish Priest of the Parish, Mr. Mark MacGrath and Mr. James Maxwell a Protestant, who gave me this account of Pyrrhus, being present. There happened to be a dark cavity under the window, which made the Purgatory-mongers at first sight believe that it was the mouth of the passage and therefore they cried for Holy Water to keep the spirits from breaking prison : and the Priest immediately left the Island in a great fright as he pretended and reported among the common people that the way into Purgatory was found out for certain, that he saw it himself and that it smelt strongly of brimstone. The rest of the Papists who stayed behind were in a great consternation, but Mr. Maxwell not being so credulous desired them to have a little patience, and they would soon be convinced of their error which accordingly fell out : for after digging a little deeper they found that it was a cellar window : whereupon Ludovicus Pyrrhus ceased from searching any more and returned to his native country. Among the rubbish they found a little bell which is now in the College of Dublin : and an image which is now said to be the image of Caoranach and is kept in the lesser Island for the satisfaction of the pilgrims. But the pretended passage into Purgatory being (as hath been already said) removed from this into a lesser Island commonly called St. Patrick's Purgatory : and this feigned removal having drawn the pilgrims thither for the purgation of their sins : and it being at present, as it hath been for several centuries, a place of great superstition and idolatry."

There was a Protestant rector of Templecarne in the seventeen-eighties, the Rev. Philip Skelton, famous for philanthropy and authorship. He wrote a rather racy account of the Lough Derg pilgrimage. It includes the detail that pilgrims making the night vigil were armed with long pins to stick into one another should need arise to ward off sleep with violence. He tells us that great criminals making the pilgrimage were given an additional penance :

" They sometimes add an extraordinary exposure or two in cases uncommonly criminal, such as setting the delinquents to roost on the beams that go across the Chapels with their breasts sticking through the broken places in the thatch : and here the women are often placed as well as the men while the congregation is beneath employed in prayer."

Skelton is the only authority, so far as I know, on whom this curious information rests. I beg leave to doubt it.

William Carleton, the county Tyrone novelist, opened his literary career and established his fame by means of a scurrilous attack on the Lough Derg pilgrimage. Fleas and general wretchedness were the characteristics of the pilgrimage, as described by him, and he tells a long, involved story of how he was villainously robbed on his way home from Lough Derg by another pilgrim, a gipsy woman, or shuler, who was a notorious character of the district, and who had made the pilgrimage with every appearance of intense devotion.

Carleton was a Catholic and says that he had intended to go on for the priesthood until his eyes were opened at Lough Derg. A great number of the writers who attack the pilgrimage are incidentally entertaining, but not so Carleton. It is difficult to read him without irritation. " The Lough Derg Pilgrim " was his first appearance in print ; he published it in a Protestant journal called *The Christian Examiner and Church of Ireland Magazine*, which was edited by the Rev. Caesar Otway, a clergyman noted for his bigotry. Carleton's essay was balm to this editor's soul. But the writer himself had had no scruple in turning the ancient devotion of his own people into a subject of satire and ridicule. In view of the history of St. Patrick's Purgatory during the preceding two hundred years, this was an essay most acceptable to Protestant Ireland. Carleton's literary success was assured from that moment. He was never to lack either patrons or a public. When he was fifty-four he was granted an annual pension of £200 through the efforts of Lord John Russell and he thus became independent of the incalculable vagaries of publishers, acceptances, advances and royalties. He became a powerful writer, master alike of humour and pathos, who enjoyed wide publicity in his lifetime. His attack on the pilgrimage is, for all those reasons, the only damaging one.

Carleton is still the boast of county Tyrone and his cult is strong among Ulster Catholics. They would not find pleasing the views just expressed. When Canon O'Connor in his history of St. Patrick's Purgatory, touched with considerably more restraint on Carleton's behaviour, he received a letter from Dr. Murray, Maynooth professor, in which he said :—

> " I on yesterday entirely forgot communicating some very interesting information regarding William Carleton, and in reference to the L. Derg tale— information of which I am now the only living repository, having had it partly from his old school-fellow, F. James Smith. There can be no doubt that grave abuses existed in those old days. The great blemish in the tale is from the ' suppressio veri ' and the paragraphs written, not by Carleton himself, but by Caesar Otway. I will, before you come to a second edition, think of some way by which your censure of Carleton may be, not with-drawn, but softened."

Canon O'Connor, in his second edition, printed that letter as a footnote, explaining that Dr. Murray died not long afterwards, without having sent him the promised information. I have quoted the letter as an illustration of the strong cult of Carleton that exists, even among Catholics. It is of course obvious to the average reader that numerous passages in " The Lough Derg Pilgrim " were interpolated by a Protestant of the most bigoted kind. Even an apostate Catholic would not have used that phrasing. Carleton was dishonourable to allow this hotch-potch to be printed over his name in a Protestant journal. It is behaviour difficult to " explain " in a creditable way.

It is regrettable that, among writers hostile to the pilgrimage, one has to include a Catholic divine, the historian Dr. John Lanigan. He came to the erroneous conclusion that the Purgatory was never heard of until the Canons Regular of St. Augustine took up residence on Saints' Island " in the eleventh century." Lanigan does not write against the pilgrimage proper, but against the popular view of its origin, which he found he could not historically confirm. It has to be added that Lanigan himself is by no means in the front rank of historians.

Caesar Otway, Carleton's first patron, wrote several interesting guide-books. In his *Sketches of Donegal*, he describes Lough Derg with such a deeply prejudiced eye that, unconsciously, he achieves humour :—

> " Lough Derg under my feet, the Lake, the shores, the mountains, the accompaniments of all sorts presented the very landscape of desolation : its waters expanding in their highland solitude amidst a wide waste of moors without one green spot to refresh the eye, without a house or tree, all mournful in the brown hue of its far-stretching bogs and the grey uniformity of its rocks : the surrounding mountains even partook of the sombre character of the place : their forms without grandeur, their ranges continuous and without elevation. The Lake itself was certainly as fine as rocky shores and numerous islands could make it : but it was compassed with such dreariness : it was deformed so much by its purgatorial Island that really the whole prospect before me struck my mind with a sense of painfulness and I said to myself : I am already in Purgatory."

It will be remembered that the Act of Queen Anne, prohibiting the pilgrimage to Lough Derg under the severest penalties of a fine, or a public whipping, was passed in the year 1704. Ten years later, the Catholic Bishop of that Diocese, Hugh MacMahon, paid a secret visit to Lough Derg and sent an account of it to Rome. This letter is extraordinary comment on the legal prohibition of the pilgrimage :

> " From the beginning of June to the end of August, there crowd each year (to it) from all parts even the most remote of this kingdom, thousands of men and women of every age and condition, who there spend nine days, living on one meal each day of oaten bread and water. They rest upon the cold

ground, walk barefoot, and their feet are frequently cut and bleeding. Thrice each day do they visit the different stations over a rough path strewn with sharp pebbles, a considerable part of which is covered with water knee-deep. At length, on the ninth day, having first made a general confession, having expiated all the faults of their life, and being nourished with the Bread of Life, they enter before twilight a subterraneous pit, which is called the Purgatory, and here they remain four and twenty continuous hours, all the time awake and engaged in prayer, without any refreshment either of food or drink. When the same hour arrives on the following day they go forth, and dip their heads thrice in the cold water. And thus is completed that pilgrimage, to which idle inventors of fables have added so many exaggerations about spectres and visions, which never had any existence save in the distorted imaginations of such story-tellers. For the three months during which this pilgrimage lasts, Masses are celebrated from dawn till midday ; confessions are heard ; twice or three times each day a sermon is addressed to the people, who with copious tears, sobs, lamentations, and other marks of penance, frequently interrupt the preacher. And with such sweetness of interior grace does our most merciful Lord enrich this arduous and very austere pilgrimage, that they who before appeared obdurate and plunged in the mire of vice, come to feel the strongest stings of compunction. Nor are they satisfied with approaching this island once or twice ; for I have found in this diocese persons who made the pilgrimage as often as fourteen times. The plenary indulgence accorded by the Holy Father, Pope Clement X, to those visiting this pilgrimage (which will soon expire, and requires a renewal), has added no small increase to the fervour of the pious pilgrims. It is regarded by all as little short of a prodigy how this pilgrimage, though prohibited by name, in the foremost place, and under the most severe penalties by Act of Parliament, suffered little or no interruption from the bitter Scotch Calvinists living in the neighbourhood and elsewhere. When I myself visited the place, under the guise of a Dublin merchant (for under the disguise of a trader or tradesman the prelates and non-registered priests of this country generally find it necessary to conceal themselves), the Minister of that district received me very kindly. Though everywhere else throughout the kingdom the ecclesiastical functions have ceased, on account of the prevailing persecution ; in this Island, as if it were placed in another orb, the exercise of religion is free and public, which is ascribed to a special favour of Divine Providence, and to the merits of St. Patrick.

" When I was there, an English Protestant, induced by the fame of the place, and out of curiosity, came there ; and, having been moved to compunction at the sight of the penitents, forthwith abjured his heresy. The Franciscan Fathers, beyond all the other ecclesiastics who come there, labour the most strenuously. At this pilgrimage I remarked one custom (not to call it an abuse), namely that they who are about to enter the cave have Mass celebrated for them, which is always a *Missa de requiem*, just as if they were dead to the world, and ready for sepulture ; which when I was anxious to abrogate, at least on Sundays and the principal festivals, on which should be said the Mass conformable to the office, they claimed the authority of immemorial possession and of custom to the contrary, first originated, as tradition says, by St. Patrick himself ; which, being constantly asserted by learned and scrupulous men, has perplexed me, and therefore I beg to be instructed by your Eminences as to what I am to do thereon."

The name of that Protestant minister was Alexander Colhoun, a great-grandson of whom afterwards became Vice-President of the United States.

The practice of saying a Requiem Mass for those about to enter the cave persisted as late as the eighteenth century. It was a symbol of the pilgrim's complete renunciation of the world. In the fourteenth century, this symbolism was enforced by the most elaborate funereal rites, as witness the following extract, taken from a description of the pilgrimage performed by Georgius, Knight of Hungary, in 1353 :—

> "After these fifteen days of fast, the Office of the Dead is said for him morning and evening during five days as though he were dead and as though for a dead man in this manner : a bier covered with a black cloth is placed in the midst of the choir of the Church of St. Patrick and there the pilgrim, who is going to enter the Purgatory, is laid like a corpse. Priest and deacon, sub-deacon and acolytes are vested as they were wont to be vested for one dead. The full Office of the Dead is then sung aloud with cross, thurible and holy water. After this has been sung in the morning the Mass of Requiem is promptly said for him and what was said in the morning must be said and done later except the Mass. When Mass has been said, the pilgrim is absolved as though he were to be taken to the grave with bells sounded as is the custom for the dead. And the same method of singing the Mass and Office of the Dead is observed during the four subsequent days."

The pilgrim of the fourteenth century certainly made a meditation on death and judgment unique in its completeness.

Bishop Hugh MacMahon's testimony in the early eighteenth century to the value of the Franciscan effort at Lough Derg must be emphasized : " The Franciscan Fathers, beyond all the other ecclesiastics who come there, labour the most strenuously ". Nothing short of heroic service evoked that tribute. The Franciscans took up the charge of St. Patrick's Purgatory when it was the most persecuted and derided institution of the Irish Church. Fugitives themselves, they encouraged and assisted this pilgrimage when to do so meant incurring hourly danger of death. They carried it on amidst its material ruin, joining the people in an attempt to gather together for veneration the broken and scattered stones of its buildings. They were the mainstay of the pilgrimage for one hundred and fifty years, or five generations, from 1631 to 1781, not from their convent in Donegal, then ruined and abandoned, but from local glens and farmsteads where they found refuge. They were able to live on the island only during the last twenty years of that period. They finally gave up the charge in 1781, when their own numbers had been reduced by persecution to vanishing point, and when they were no longer able to spare members for the pilgrimage. But when they left the scene St. Patrick's Purgatory had undergone a new resurrection.

The history of St. Patrick's Purgatory presents a most difficult problem : the identification of the site of the historic cave of St. Patrick. It has been seen that the cave is prominently in the foreground of all that island history ; without it, the pilgrimage would at one time have been unthinkable. Here I repeat for the reader's convenience much that has already been said. Legend has it that there was a cave on Station Island before St. Patrick visited it, and that evil spirits, the dispossessed devils of Druidic worship, had made that dark pit their abode until the Saint routed them. An alternative version of the legend says that the Irish were difficult to convince on the doctrine of Hell and Purgatory and that Patrick, with a gesture that was a kind of despairing anger, traced a circle on the ground with his staff, whereupon the ring opened to reveal a pit of fire, the original " Purgatory."

The cave, anyhow, was the great feature of the

pilgrimage from earliest times until nearly the end of the eighteenth century. For hundreds of years an indispensable part of the pilgrimage rite was a twenty-four hour vigil in the cave. It was in the cave that the Knight Owen saw the after-life, and his experience, as we have seen, set in motion a vast machinery of fantasy. The earliest accounts of the cave represent it as a kind of pit with steps leading down to a considerable depth. Later, this interior hole seems to have been covered up with a flagstone, and there was used only the cave at ground level, L-shaped, one large room giving entry into a much smaller one.

This legendary cave, so precious in the eyes of the early Irish Church, was on Station Island, and around it were grouped the beehive cells of the first Celtic anchorites, a few of whom always dwelt here, though their monastery proper was on the adjoining Saints' Island. The remains of those beehive cells form the penitential " beds " over which the pilgrim walks to-day. From very earliest times, the constant number of those cells seems to have been five ; at least since the seventeenth century, they have been dedicated respectively to Saints Brigid, Catherine, Columcille, Brendan, Dabheoc and Molaise (who shared one cell), and Patrick. The cell of Dabheoc and Molaise was closely joined to that of Patrick, forming a kind of double ring ; that double ring remains to-day, but the dedication to Patrick has disappeared, while Dabheoc and Molaise each appropriate one link as it were in that double ring. This double ring of stone is described in the Leaflet of Instructions issued to present-day pilgrims as " the large Penitential Bed."

The Florentine pilgrim, Antonio Mannini, gave us a description of the cave as he found it in the year 1411, worth repeating because it is so refreshing in its exactness and verisimilitude :—

> " The place is three feet wide, nine feet long and high enough for a man to kneel but not to stand upright. It is exactly like a sepulchre, for it is

vaulted overhead and lies towards the south,
that is, there is a niche about three feet long in the
direction of the Chapel, in which the Prior had
told me to remain and wait, saying my prayers
the while."

Unfortunately, the Florentine does not tell us the exact
site of the cave in relation to the penal beds. However,
most of the accounts of other notable pilgrims concur
with his in saying that the Prior and assistant priests
lived in a monastery on Saints' Island, where the pilgrim
apparently performed his preliminary fast ; he was then
rowed over to Station Island, where he was locked up
in the renowned cave for the vigil.

Then came the Dutch monk from Eymstadt in 1494,
throwing confusion on the scene in every sense of the
word. In his case he was not conducted into a cave
to have a door locked behind him, but " he was let down
by the Sacristan by a rope into a deep Pit ". This is the
first time there is mention of a rope having been used
to put a pilgrim into the cave. One is inclined to
sympathise with the Dutch monk who was so cavalierly
treated. As described already, he had no " experience "
and was exceedingly annoyed by morning. When he
left Ireland he had a complaint lodged with the Pope,
who ordered the cave to be closed up. This order was
carried out in the year 1497. The *Annals of Ulster*
record the event and say that the reason the cave was
closed up was that " This was not the Purgatory Patrick
got from God although they were, everyone, visiting it."

It is clear from the Dutch monk's account that he was
not taken to Station Island at all. For some reason not
easy to fathom the Canons Regular then in charge of the
pilgrimage were no longer taking pilgrims across to the
real Purgatory, but were putting them instead into a
substitute cave on Saints' Island. It was this substitute
cave that was closed by Papal decree.

The closing of the substitute cave on Saints' Island
had no adverse effect on the pilgrimage. Its continuity

was preserved and, all in the same lifetime, Rome favoured it with indulgences. But where now were the pilgrims making the vigil ? They evidently resumed use of the original cave on Station Island, because undoubtedly that is the cave described in the records of later pilgrims.

In the *Florilegium* of Messingham, published in 1587, there is a most interesting discussion of the cave :

" Some are of opinion, that the cave, or pit, shown by Christ our Lord to St. Patrick, is either unknown or invisible, or, at least, is not that into which the pilgrims go, and are shut up for twenty-four hours ; but either lies hid underneath, or a few paces from it. So, according to ancient tradition have I been informed by the Reverend John Gaffney, abbot of Leathra ; and John M'Kegan, a priest, a septuagenarian. Others consider that the place is altogether unknown, and will not be seen by man until the end of the world ; like the sepulchre of Moses, and the Ark of the Covenant among the ancient Hebrews previous to their return from Babylon. And this last is the opinion of Father Eugene Duffy, a Franciscan, and a man of wellknown piety, as I have been told by Torny Mulchonry, an aged antiquary. Whether Duffy, Gaffney, Conry, Kegan and others be correct in this relation, which nevertheless, is not the opinion most generally received, I shall say nothing at present ; but grave men consider that we ought not rashly to abandon the common belief that prevails among so many, namely, that the cave, covered in like a low vault, which is seen in the Island of Lough Derg, is the true site of the pit that we seek."

It is certain that the plain people of Ireland who formed the majority of pilgrims did not abandon that belief. When the Government made up its mind in 1632 to destroy the pilgrimage to St. Patrick's Purgatory,

we have seen that the cave was the very special concern
of the destroyers. They considered it the focal point of
the whole devotion, so they saw to it that it was thoroughly
dug up on all sides and then filled in to ground level,
so as completely to obliterate it.

The cave then filled in was popularly believed to be
at least on the site of the original cave. When the
pilgrimage was furtively resumed, under the very nose
of the persecutors, a substitute shelter built of loose
stones was hastily put up to serve for the vigil. This
rude shelter was styled the Cave. Later another one
was added to house the numbers wishing to make the
vigil at the same time, so that presently one is confused
by mention of several caves. Yet it was, after all, but a
natural evolution. There are extant several maps of
Station Island engraved subsequent to the demolition of
1632, when the pilgrimage had been resumed : that of
Sir James Ware (in *De Hibernia et antiquitatibus ejus*,
1658), that of Father Thomas Carve (in *Lyra Hibernica*,
1666) and that of Edward Ledwich (in *Antiquities of
Ireland*, 1790). The substitute cave is marked on those
maps and all concur in placing it north of St. Mary's
Church, between St. Brigid's Bed and the eastern edge
of the island. It is certain that the penitential " Beds "
of the Saints have occupied from time immemorial the
same position that they hold to-day ; and St. Mary's
Church has been on relatively the same site. It seems
likely that, when an overground shelter was erected for
pilgrims, after the 1632 destruction, it was placed on the
site of the historic cave that had been filled in. According
to the maps referred to, that location was on ground
now occupied by the present bell-tower. Canon O'Connor,
in his history of " St. Patrick's Purgatory," has a note
on this :—

> " the cave was situated near the present campanile
> (and this is confirmed by the remains of a narrow
> building, corresponding with the dimensions of the
> cave, which may be seen at either side of the

campanile, and which tradition points to as part of the cave) . . . . "

To-day there is no trace of such remains, but when the present bell-tower was being built some excavation became necessary and the late Canon McKenna then claimed to have discovered on this site the walls of the original cave.

That place of wonder, terror, piety and—let it be conceded—superstition is now completely hidden from the pilgrims' view by a high grassy mound. In the very circumscribed island space of three-quarters of an acre, this elevated and open ground is much favoured by pilgrims. During the crowded " seasons " they cluster thickly on it for brief intervals of repose, chatting in subdued voices, or sitting in meditative aloofness, undisturbed by either sulphurous exhalations or any immediate expectation of apocalyptic visions.

The pilgrimage authorities put an end to all doubts and difficulties connected with the pilgrimage when they closed up the cave, or caves, in the year 1789 and made a ruling that henceforth the vigil was to be made in the Church. The reason given for this new ruling was that the caves had become dangerous to pilgrims because of the large number that used to crowd into them at the same time ; the provision of a roomy site for the vigil had become essential for the proper conduct of the pilgrimage. When even the overflow caves on Station Island were abolished, the miracle-mongers received their final death-blow. Without the accessory of an eerie cavern the spinning of fantasies became impossible. From that date, the word " Purgatory " in the title of the pilgrimage is held to be descriptive of its penitential nature only and of its usefulness in providing a means for making satisfaction for sin.

Episodes full of human interest are constantly occurring at Lough Derg, but they are usually the secrets of in-

H

dividuals. The pilgrimage once witnessed the closing scene of a great romance between Turlough O'Carolan, poet and composer, called " The Last of the Bards," and his first love, Bridget Cruise. Turlough was son of a county Meath farmer and great-grandson of a chieftain. He contracted smallpox as a youth and became blind in consequence, but this did not prevent him from developing his special gifts of music and poetry. He became a noted harpist and was a welcome guest in the houses of well-to-do people, whom he entertained with his music, and many of whom still live in his verses.

The first love of this man's life was a certain Bridget Cruise. He wrote his first poem in her praise and composed several songs for her. But Bridget's parents strongly disapproved and would not agree to her marriage with O'Carolan. The couple had to separate. The bard afterwards married a girl named Mary Maguire, with whom he was happy. Twenty years after his enforced separation from Bridget, the harpist made the Lough Derg pilgrimage. On his return to the mainland, as usually happens, a group of other pilgrims, who were waiting for their turn to be ferried across, gathered around to assist at the disembarkation. O'Carolan, like the others, took a friendly hand in his in order to step from the boat and was seen to be seized with powerful emotion as he cried out, " This is the hand of Bridget Cruise ! " No word had been spoken but, after twenty years, recognition by touch had been instantaneous. This episode has passed into the national songs of Ireland. Among others, Samuel Lover was inspired by it.

The end of the eighteenth-century history of Lough Derg is sadly remembered because of a particularly bad boating accident. It happened on the 12th July, 1795, at a period when the transport of pilgrims was not under the control of the church authorities. In those days a " shebeen " was kept near the ferry and on special occasions such as the "Twelfth," poteen circulated freely among the Protestant boatmen. The day happened to be Sunday and an unusual number of people came to be ferried across, many of them being local residents anxious just to hear Mass on the island. As a boat was being loaded with passengers at eleven o'clock, an elderly man arrived at the shore and urgently signalled to his son to come away with him. The young man protested: he was fasting; he was intent on making the pilgrimage. But the father insisted strongly that he had had an extremely alarming dream and that his son would have to postpone the pilgrimage, at least for a day. Both left together.

Ninety-three people were then crowded into an old and leaky boat, despite their protests. The fact that the boatmen were drunk made the passengers still more uneasy. In those days, ill-treatment of pilgrims on the part of those who made money out of them was taken almost as a matter of course. The boat pushed off. The distance from mainland to island can be covered in ten minutes. Halfway across, however, the boat was seen to be taking in water. The boatmen were in too stupid a condition to be able to quiet the passengers' fears. Between Friars' Island and Station Island such confusion developed on board that the boat capsized. It is said that a dozen more strokes of the oars would have brought it to safety. Pilgrims grouped on the island wharf, watching the boat's arrival, were petrified with dismay to see the water suddenly filled with struggling human beings. Ninety pilgrims were drowned in less than ten feet of water; there were only three survivors. There were boats at hand, and presence of mind, even among the onlookers, could have averted the tragedy.

About twenty of the victims were buried on Friars' Island, where fir-trees on a mound show their grave to-day. Numbers of others were buried in a corporate grave in Templecarne churchyard, marked by an ancient memorial cross taken from Saints' Island. Some twenty or more of those unfortunate pilgrims, however, had travelled

from Connacht, and their relatives arrived to carry
home the dead. They were poor people and local tradition
has it that they carried the dead bodies on their backs
all the long and mountainous journey to their homes in
the west.

The new liberty enjoyed by the pilgrimage towards
the end of the eighteenth century expressed itself in two
ways : in a great floraison of building, to be described
later ; and, unexpectedly, in a marked lessening of the
pilgrimage severity. There appeared in 1824 a book by
an unknown author, describing *Excursions in Ulster*,
which included a description of Lough Derg. This writer
supplies the detail that the rite, which was originally a
fast of fifteen days, then of nine, had now been reduced
to a period of six days. A three-day period finds its first
mention about the same time. This is revealed in the
Diary of Bishop Blake of Dromore, under the date of
April 25th, 1825 :—

> " I received to-day a letter from Dr. Kernan, dated
> Carrickmacross, April 5. In it he requests that I
> apply to His Eminence Cardinal della Somaglia,
> for a continuance of the indulgence granted to
> the Island of Lough Derg, to which hundreds of
> Catholics flock every year with the express per-
> mission and approbation of their respective pastors,
> and after having complied with their Paschal duty,
> in order to do penance and make a retreat of three,
> six, or nine days."

A book entitled *Tour through Ireland*, by Henry
Inglis, appeared in 1834 and gave a description of the
Lough Derg pilgrimage. This writer says that in that
year the pilgrim had the option of doing the penance for
three, six, or nine consecutive days, or even for fifteen
days as a special favour.

The usual period of the pilgrimage is now three days.
Permission to make it for six days is still frequently

asked and conceded ; nine days have become rare, and fifteen days altogether exceptional. I heard some years ago of a young girl from Monaghan who asked so persistently for permission to make a fifteen-day pilgrimage that she was allowed to do so. She carried it through successfully and left in good health and spirits. A young man sought the same permission shortly afterwards. After four days, he became disturbed—and disturbed others—by visions, so he was sent home.

VIII. THE NINETEENTH CENTURY

THE Statute of Queen Anne, passed in 1704, forbidding the Lough Derg pilgrimage under severe penalties, became a dead letter in effect long before the passing of Catholic Emancipation. Actually five reigns of British monarchs intervened—between Anne and the good, if bigoted, Victoria—before the obsolete ruling was repealed from the Statutes in 1871.

The Irish people, however, were very little affected by the Nay and Yea of British Queens. They felt the spirit of freedom long before it was officially conceded. It manifested itself chiefly in buildings.

Crowds are the feature of this island history during the first half of the nineteenth century, waves of people landing on the place all through the ten weeks of the pilgrimage season, while those in charge were forever striving to cope in an orderly manner with this pressure of people. Imagine what conditions were like without adequate housing arrangements for those crowds. There were days when boat-loads of pilgrims had to be rowed back, disappointed, to the mainland, and wait there for a day or two perhaps, because there was not room for them on Station Island. Sometimes human beings were congregated on that rock as thickly as colonies of puffins. Recall that the entire area of the island is less than an acre and that much of this space was always necessarily occupied by buildings. Huts, ranging in number from twelve to twenty, were used in the early nineteenth century for the accommodation of pilgrims. Each hut provided sleeping quarters for about ten people. The year 1846 was memorable for its number of pilgrims, 30,000 being the total for the season. There had been some terrific days during those ten weeks. There was a certain day when thirteen hundred pilgrims landed on the island ; this is said to be the record for any single day in the nineteenth century. On the night not devoted to the vigil, those thirteen hundred had to occupy the sleeping accommodation of two hundred. A great number of the pilgrims used in those days to sleep on the floor of St. Mary's Church, or in the confessionals, or in the boats. Thus the incidental physical hardship experienced on the island could be nearly as severe as the rigours of the pilgrimage.

To understand the fortitude of pilgrims during the period under review, one must remember that there was no road to the lake. Until 1877 the pilgrims had to pick their way as best they could over a mere track through bogland which, after rain, was liable to become a morass. A traveller need only look at the country to right and left of the existing road to-day, on the near approaches to the lake, in order to have a good idea of the former pilgrimage track. About the year 1877, the landlord of the district, Sir John Leslie, made part of the present road from Pettigo for his own purposes. Later he completed it as far as the lake. This road is to-day the principal approach to the lake. The landlord nominally kept the last mile of the road in repair, but often pilgrims found it in such a condition they had to patch it up themselves with sods and rubble before they could walk on it. The prior also used to give his quota of assistance to pilgrims by draining the most flooded parts of the route and strewing bundles of heather in the ruts and holes. There are people still living to-day who remember when there was not even a bridge over the river at Brennan's Hotel in Pettigo. Professional " strong men " used to take up their station there and carry pilgrims over at a charge of a penny a time.

There is a second road direct from Donegal, crossing the mountain to the lake, where it touches the shore at " Donegal Point," close to Saints' Island. Yet a third road runs from Castlederg past Killeter, through the district of Aughyarren, joining up with the Pettigo road about a mile from the lake shore.

There is still indicated on ordnance maps an ancient

road leading from Pettigo and Templecarne, towards the
Owenea river, across Ballymacavanny to the present
ferry. Even in the Middle Ages, a well-defined track,
chiefly constructed of stepping-stones laid together in
regular order, led all the way from Lough Erne to Lough
Derg. Portions of this ancient track are still discoverable,
though it has not been used for hundreds of years, and
the greater part of it is completely obliterated under
heather and peat.

Lough Derg's second spring was really marked by the
erection of a chapel in 1763 by the Franciscan Father
Anthony O'Doherty, dedicated to the Blessed Virgin
Mary of the Angels. When the cave was closed up in
1789 and the vigil transferred to the church, a second
larger church, dedicated to Saint Patrick, was in readiness to replace the cave. From that year onwards two
churches were always maintained on the island : St.
Patrick's (now replaced by the Basilica), where all the
pilgrims heard Mass and made the night vigil ; and St.
Mary's (on the same site as the present church of that
name) where assistant priests, or priests making the
pilgrimage, said Mass and where Confessions were,
and still are, heard.

Building was constantly going on on the island in
an effort to make the accommodation, both for prayer
and sleeping purposes, adequate for the throngs who
made the pilgrimage. It was a period of extremely bad
building, which always proves the most expensive kind.
St. Mary's is the worst example of this. It was found
unsuitable even for its secondary purposes by the year
1813, when it was pulled down, and a new church,
with the same dedication, was put up almost on the
same site. This church was again enlarged in 1835.
Although it was extensively repaired in 1860, it was
pulled down again ten years later and a new church,
always with the same dedication, was put up in the same
place.

Meanwhile the same cobbling went on with St. Patrick's.
Seven years after it was built, it had to be re-roofed and

slated ; an aisle was added in 1835 ; its interior was reconstructed and its galleries removed in 1860 ; it was again improved and repaired in 1878.

Work on a suitable presbytery for the officiating priests had been going on simultaneously with this church building. A new house for the clergy had been built in 1816, re-modelled in 1860, and practically re-built in 1864. The present presbytery, standing almost on the edge of the jetty, was built by Canon Smith about 1907. Though small and simple, it has a great deal of character. It is the house nearest to the mainland and its white-washed walls gleam familiarly from afar. The house that was formerly a presbytery is now used as sleeping accommodation for the hostel attendants ; its kitchen and diningroom are used by certain pilgrims ; five or six beds in it are used as overflow accommodation.

It may well be asked what reason can account for the timorousness that prevented the pilgrimage authorities from building nobly and enduringly in the eighteenth and nineteenth centuries ? The reason for this diffidence was not so much poverty as insecurity of tenure, which has, as everyone knows, a paralysing effect when improvements are in question.

The discomfort suffered by pilgrims for want of sufficient accommodation especially during the memorable season of 1846, inspired a ferryman of that time, named Daniel Campbell, with the idea of building a hostel on the island the following year. He received the Prior's permission and set to work. The walls of the building were almost raised when the land-lord's agent became aware of the activity. He im-mediately called on Campbell, putting under his nose for signature a document undertaking to pay the land-lord a certain rent for the site. Campbell would not agree, as he well understood that to do this would prejudice the Catholic claim to ownership of the island. He refused to sign. The agent countered by preventing the transport of any more building material across the lake. Work on the hostel had to be suspended and, as chance would have it, was never again resumed. The half completed walls were left standing for twenty-three years, and were taken down again in 1870.

It took thirty-six years of litigation before the impediment of uncertain tenure was removed from Lough Derg and the Prior was free to take command of the situation and re-order the pilgrimage in a fitting way. Incidentally this was perhaps the most famous case of ecclesiastical ownership that ever arose in Ireland. The legal battle, tenaciously fought and honourably won, is not the least absorbing chapter in the island history.

The cloud of disputed ownership first settled on Lough Derg in 1596, when Donough Magrath made that historic surrender to Queen Elizabeth of all the lands around the lake (known as Termon Magrath) " for the purpose of reducing the lands to English tenure." The document of surrender embodied the re-grant of the same lands to Donough for life and afterwards to his heirs male. He was but one of the many victims of the " Surrender and Re-Grant " fiction. It all looked so simple : he had but to sign a brief document surrendering his entire estates to England, when the Crown would immediately hand them back to him as a gift, with far more security to his title than heretofore; he would have to pay a nominal little rental, in return for which he could claim protection from a mighty military power.

In Donough's case, his surrender was complicated by the fact that he had never been sole owner of the land he handed over. It has been explained that the patrimony allotted to the upkeep of the monastery on Saints' Island had been vested jointly in the Magraths, hereditary keepers of the property, and in the ecclesiastical rulers of the district, or of the diocese as it later became. The latter were of course ignored in the surrender. They had no option but to bear with this material loss, all excepting less than an acre of that vast estate, namely, Station Island in Lough Derg, whose ownership they persisted in claiming with a most inconvenient tenacity.

According to the Patent Rolls, the lands of Termon Magrath, including Lough Derg, were granted in 1610 to James, eldest son of Miler Magrath, and this James Magrath later made over his lease to James Spottiswoode, his father's successor in the Protestant See of Clogher. Apparently it was not zeal for religion alone that had caused this worthy to be so actively engaged in the destruction of the Lough Derg shrine. He had a shrewd eye also to material recompense and he was in fact rewarded by the ownership of all the surrounding lands, as recorded in the Auchinlech manuscript :—

> " (Dr. Spottiswoode) recovered also other lands, his predecessor, Bishop Montgomerie, was never in possession of ; as, namely, the Isle of Devenish, from the Lord Hastings ; the greatest part of the Island of Inishmore, from Sir Ralph Goore, Baronet ; the lands of Termonmagrath from James Magrath."

Thus Termon Magrath became part of the extensive Protestant See lands and devolved in due time to Bishop John Leslie, when he was installed in the See of Clogher in 1661. This was the origin of the present Leslie family's connection with Lough Derg.

Bishop John Leslie bequeathed the lease of Termon Magrath to his son, Charles, who thereafter paid to the Protestant Church body an annual rental of forty pounds a year for it. I do not know by what manœuvring he made a private bequest of part of the See lands. The Protestant See of Clogher became united to that of Armagh in 1834 by Act of Parliament. The descendants of Charles Leslie, who were then living in Glasslough, Co. Monaghan, were all this time paying the rental and renewing the lease of Termon Magrath. They legally ratified their ownership by purchasing in 1836 the fee-simple of this holding for the sum of £4,508. Thus it came about that the Leslies acquired the feudal powers of the apostate Magraths.

Unaffected by those vicissitudes in the holding of the property, however, the Catholic Church all down the centuries never relinquished its claim to the ownership at least of Station Island. It did not succeed in making good that claim until 1917.

Before the present hospices for men and women were built, the only accommodation for pilgrims was in the cabins. The fact that the cabin-keepers rented small farms from the Leslies on the mainland made the position more complicated. After Campbell had made that abortive attempt to build a hospice, the agent of the Leslie estate made a determined effort to get his tenants to make their tenancy of the mainland farms and their tenancy of the island cabins into a single agreement, both tenancies to be covered by a single rent receipt. Had the tenants agreed, this arrangement would of course have greatly prejudiced the Catholic claim to ownership of the island. They refused, on the Prior's advice. Threatened with eviction from both holdings, they still refused.

One of the cabin-keepers, whose name was William Mulligan, eventually gave in to the agent's pressure and sold to him for the sum of £12 his interest in his island cabin. The agent then let it to a certain Robert Muldoon. The Prior interdicted it and, later, he rented it to a ferryman.

When the Catholic Bishop of Clogher, Dr. M'Nally, was informed of these difficulties, he sent a warning to the cabin-keepers that if any among them gave in to the unjust demands being made on them by the Leslie agent the pilgrimage would be closed down. Later, the Bishop visited Station Island, put on all his episcopal insignia and, with two priests as witnesses, he went round from cabin to cabin formally ejecting every tenant. He then reinstated the keepers at a nominal seasonal rent of one penny per cabin, for which he gave each keeper a receipt. This was a gesture which proved very useful later on. Great honour is indeed due the Clogher diocese for the determination with which they held on to their rights in Station Island. During certain critical years, the least weakness or relaxation on their part would have meant the total loss of the Island.

There was no hope of escape from this struggle. The devotion was so vigorous that the need for proper housing for the pilgrims could not be ignored. In the autumn of 1879 the then Prior, Canon James McKenna, set off on a tour of the continent to examine hostels at the famous shrines of Lourdes, Paray-le-Monial, and also Holywell in England. On his return, with the knowledge thus gained, he caused to be prepared a plan for Lough Derg hostel. This building was commenced on the island in 1880 : it consisted of two separate houses under the same roof, one for women and the other for men. No sooner were the foundations of this building laid down in 1881 than trouble began again with the landlord. One corner of the foundations had necessarily to rest on a ledge of rock, covered with water except in dry seasons. This part of the building was termed an encroachment on the bed of the lake and an infringement of the landlord's proprietary rights. Correspondence on the matter was exchanged between Sir John Leslie and the Bishop without clearing up the difficulty and finally a writ of summons was issued against the Bishop, claiming damages for trespass.

The case was called for the summer assizes at Donegal, 1881. Meanwhile the building of the hospice continued and was actually completed that summer. The Bishop secured the best legal aid available who spent months hard at work investigating and copying ancient records to prove the title of the Clogher diocese to the island. Two counsels and two barristers were engaged to defend the case. All were assembled in court on the morning of July 16th, waiting with considerable eagerness and interest for the case to be unfolded, when Sir John Leslie's counsel approached the defendant's solicitor with a proposal of settlement : to wit, that Sir John withdrew all claim to the island, and 2nd, that he was prepared to give a lease for 999 years of that portion of the

water upon which the hospice intruded, at a nominal
rental, if required. After a great deal of discussion
acting on the advice of his legal aid and of his priests
the Bishop agreed. The settlement was made a rule of
court and duly signed, the costs of each side being borne
by each side. The diocese of Clogher rose to the occasion
each parish sending in a generous subscription.

The season of 1882, following that legal victory, was
memorable for the joyfulness that seemed to invest every
the penitential exercises. The hospice was opened to
receive pilgrims who henceforth were to have, not comfort
of course, but simple and decent conditions for their
second night's stay on the island.

Ordinations took place that year on the island for
the first and only time on record. Two priests, one
destined for Toronto and the other for Wellington, New
Zealand, were ordained in St. Patrick's Church by Archbishop Lynch of Toronto. The thronging of people on
the Sunday of the Ordinations nearly rivalled certain
days of the famous 1846 season. Between visitors and
pilgrims, twelve hundred were ferried across that morning.
During this season, also, the white marble statue representing " Our Blessed Lady of Lough Derg " was
presented and unveiled.

But the truce was brief. It is true that the landlord
had verbally surrendered all claim to the island, but
curiously enough this agreement had never been ratified
in writing. The fact is that the Bishop was secretly
dissatisfied with the measure of victory, and had taken
no pains to have the settlement properly drawn up, lest
it should prejudice a better settlement which he hoped
would be made later on, either by himself or by his
successor.

A couple of years later, one of the island cabins,
occupied by a man named Thomas Muldoon, fell into
disrepair and this gave the landlord a new opening.
Whatever took place between tenant and agent, the result
was that the latter agreed to make the cabin habitable
again at his expense. During 1883, but not during the

pilgrimage season, the agent took some labourers over, partly pulled down the Muldoon cabin and rebuilt it again at a cost of £27 10s. The following season (1884) the landlord re-let this house to Thomas Muldoon at a yearly rent of £1 per year, to be paid half-yearly. Muldoon, at the same time, like all the other cabin-keepers, had to pay a nominal rent to the Bishop of the diocese. But the fact that Muldoon paid a rent to the landlord too was vexatious and obviously threatened the Catholic position. Muldoon's house soon became the fulcrum upon which this whole question was to be decided.

Thomas Muldoon died in 1910, thus bringing matters to a head. The landlord at this date was Colonel John Leslie, son of that Sir John Leslie who had been plaintiff in the legal action of 1881. Soon after the death of Thomas Muldoon the Leslie bailiff arrived on the island to take possession of the deceased man's cabin. The Prior was then Archdeacon Keown—a man not easily intimidated, fortunately for the issue of this litigation.

Faced with a difficult situation that allowed him no time to confer with anyone, he decided on strong action. This is the reply he made to the bailiff's demand note :—

> " Sanctuary of Lough Derg,
> Pettigo, Co. Donegal.
> 11th June, 1910.

" Mr. George Crichton of Pettigo has just shown me a note which he received this morning from Mr. B. M. Skelton, Estate Agent, Glasslough, in which Mr. Skelton claims on behalf of Colonel Leslie the right of appropriating the house on Station Island, Lough Derg, which was formerly occupied by the late Thomas Muldoon.

" I have informed Mr. Crichton that the owner-ship of the soil of Station Island, Lough Derg, and of all the houses on the Island belongs to the Roman Catholic Bishop of Clogher, and that, as the Bishop's representative on the Island, I cannot permit anyone to interfere with, or to exercise any rights of ownership over the Island or any houses situated on the Island, that further I cannot permit anyone to land on the Island for the purpose of exercising such alleged ownership.

(Signed) PATRICK KEOWN, P.P.
Prior of the Sanctuary of Lough Derg."

The bailiff retreated with that letter. Silence ensued for the rest of the pilgrimage season. Indeed, the silence remained unbroken for six years.

The following year the Prior gave the tenancy of the disputed cabin to Robert Muldoon, brother of the deceased Thomas. It passed from him to Mary Muldoon, the last surviving member of that family, who died in 1916. She bequeathed the cabin to Archdeacon Keown, a rather ironical bequest, because the beneficiary denied the right of bequeathal. As representative of the Bishop of Clogher, owner of the island, he claimed the ownership of the house of right. He gave the tenancy to John Flood in 1916.

Colonel Leslie had by this time become Sir John Leslie. He claimed the ownership of the house under an agreement made with Thomas Muldoon, brother of Mary Muldoon and previous occupier ; more serious still he claimed the house as part of his ownership of the whole island. On the 10th May, 1916, two Notices to Quit were brought to the island by the district civil bill officer : one of these notices was personally served on the Prior ; the other was posted on the door of the Muldoon house. The pilgrimage season opened and closed without further incident.

Early the following year, the same officer personally claimed possession of the Muldoon house from the Prior, who refused to give it up. A summons was served on the latter the following month, and once more the disputed ownership of Station Island was called before the

Courts for settlement. The case was listed for hearing at the Quarter Sessions in Donegal on 30th May, 1917. This time there was to be no last-minute agreement out of court.

The pilgrimage season had opened and numbers were already gathered on the island, when the Prior prepared to leave in order to attend the court. He explained the whole matter to the pilgrims and asked them to keep special watch before the Blessed Sacrament until the hearing of the case was concluded. When the Prior walked down to the landing-stage, with the pilgrimage books under his arm for production in court, he was surrounded by good wishes and promises of prayers. All present assembled to see him off and a cheer was raised as the oars dipped.

The hearing of the evidence took two days and, from many points of view, it was one of the most interesting cases ever tried in Ireland. The plaintiff was a baronet and a Protestant, the principal defendant a dignitary of the Catholic Church, against whom a civil bill of ejectment had been brought. The ostensible subject of dispute between these two gentlemen was a poor cabin, crudely built, which neither party of course really wanted for itself. Everyone knew that the real issue to be decided was the ownership of the island on which the cabin stood.

Mr. Reid, solicitor, Ballyshannon, appeared for Sir John Leslie. Mr. Lardner conducted the case for Archdeacon Keown. It was heard in Donegal before Judge Cooke, K.C.

Mr. Reid, in seeking to establish Sir John Leslie's claim, made the following statement :—

" As far back as the 29th August, 1680, the estate surrounding this (Station) Island was by the then called Consistory conveyed to Charles Leslie,

I

a predecessor of ours, of Leslie Castle, in the County of Monaghan . . . . The six lodging houses (on Station Island) are in the hands of tenants of ours who have farms on the mainland. These tenants are rated for these houses. Muldoon's house was rated at the annual value of 10s. of which 6d. was paid. In or about the year 1883, the then Sir John Leslie, who has since died, entered on the Island, and at the request of Thomas Muldoon, he took his house partly down, then rebuilt it at a cost of £27 10s. Afterwards, (1884) Sir John entered into an Agreement with Thomas Muldoon, and under it Sir John let the house on Station Island to Thomas Muldoon at a yearly rent of £1 per year, to be paid half-yearly. His successors continued to pay that rent regularly down to September, 1915, when the last payment was made by Mary Muldoon, who has since died. At her death in January, 1916, she left her house to Archdeacon Keown."

Mr. Lardner—" We don't acknowledge that we claim any benefit under the will. Our claim is that the Island is our property, and we say that the letting made by Sir John Leslie was not a true letting, but an attempt on the part of the Leslie family to go back on an arrangement made prior to the letting, and also an attempt to get the Island into their own hands."

Mr. Reid—" Canon Keown refused to recognise our rights in any shape or form : he repudiated us ; he said that he had nothing to do with us . . . . I think it well to mention that the Ferry has nothing to do with Station Island. From the year 1847 Agreements have been regularly entered into letting that Ferry for the year to the Floods (a Pettigo family). The last Agreement was signed by Mr. John Flood on 23rd May, 1917."

Mr. Reid then concluded by formally claiming on behalf of the plaintiffs the proprietorship of the house in dispute.

Mr. Lardner (Counsel for Archdeacon Keown) said :
' I thought that this was purely a claim in respect of the
mall cabin which was occupied by Muldoon, but it is
quite evident from the way in which plaintiff's case has
been presented that it is an attempt to set up a claim on
the part of Sir John Leslie to the ownership of what is now
known as Station Island, and from the point of view of
the ecclesiastical authorities of the Diocese of Clogher it
is a serious and responsible matter which must be
ought by them in the strongest possible way.

" Your Honour may perhaps take an interest in the
history of the pilgrimage. It claims to be and
authority is found for it—both in history and tradition—
the oldest and most venerated pilgrimage of its kind
in the civilised world. Its tradition dates back to the
time of St. Patrick, but in any event mention is
made of it in the Annals of the Four Masters and
right down through all the ages since the 11th century,
by historians, poets and writers, as well as in the State
papers of the time. Notwithstanding what the conditions
were or what happened the faithful never ceased coming
to what was known as St. Patrick's Purgatory, not alone
from all parts of Ireland and the British Isles, but also
from the Continent of Europe, and some of those who
came in the olden days were so much impressed by what
they had seen and what they had to pass through that
they went to the British Authorities—the English
authorities of those days—to get a certificate to prove
that they had done the pilgrimage.

" What is Lough Derg ? It is what it once was
described by one of the writers who were charmed
with it, as :

A fragment fallen from ancient time,
That floateth there unchanged.

It formed the theme of some of the finest writings and
poetry by Ariosto, Dante, Calderon, and in later years
by M'Carthy and M'Gee. All through the ages the
authority and dominion over Station Island has been
exercised—invariably exercised—by the Prior for the

time being of Lough Derg. At one time it was under the
control of the monks, but they were driven out.

" Attempts were made to stop the pilgrimage by Acts of
Parliament. I am told, and I am glad to hear it, that at the
present time there is no attempt to interfere with it, that
there is nothing but a desire to assist it in every way
possible. Any other attitude on the part of Sir John Leslie
would surprise me. As an ordinary citizen and not as an
advocate I must ask myself why he really brought these
proceedings in respect of a barren rock which is of no
value to any person except on account of its traditions,
its associations, and its sacred connections ? The Prior
has no doubt as to what his rights are, because the
ecclesiastical authorities have spent lavishly on it
to meet the conveniences of those who come from
all parts of the world. It is not a small thing. The
pilgrims are coming in growing numbers, and it has a
world-wide reputation. In the olden days there were
30,000 pilgrims. Last year the number of pilgrims ex-
ceeded 10,000. That seems to be a matter which the
landlord cannot complain about, because he has an
interest in the ferry rights.

" The pilgrimage opens each year on the first day of
June and lasts to the 15th of August, and during that
time a priest of the Diocese of Clogher, duly authorised
by the Bishop for the time being, resides with
assistants on the Island in what is known as the
Prior's house, and he controls and directs the
pilgrimage. There are at the present time five cabins,
or what were formerly known as cabins, and now referred
to as boarding or lodging houses. In addition to the
Prior's house, there are two large Hospices and two
large Churches on the Island. At the termination of the
pilgrimage, the entire place is closed up. The cabin
holders, the Prior, his assistants, and the staff who look
after the comforts of the pilgrims leave the Island and
go back to their homes on the mainland.

" I may say at once that the reason Archdeacon Keown
resists this claim is because he claims as representing the

Bishop for the time being that he is the owner, that he has acquired a title to it, and any doubt about that title has been set at ease by an action in 1881 referred to only in passing by Mr. Reid. In order to simplify matters, I would ask your Honour to look at the map (produced). The action was brought in respect of the building of the Hospice which projects on the bed of the Lake and the soil of the Island, and it was for £200 damages for trespass on the bed of the Lake and for removing portion of the soil of the Island. At the last moment a Consent was entered into certifying that the defendant agreed to take a lease at a nominal rent in respect of the portion of the bed of the Lake where had laid the foundation of the hospice. I will rely very strongly on that, because it shows what Sir John Leslie's position was in respect of the ownership of the soil of the Island.

" I will press the matter further and show to your Honour, first by documentary evidence, that the cabin holder from time immemorial, and certainly prior to 1881, paid a yearly rent in respect of this particular cabin, and I am going to prove that that money was paid each year by the cabin holder, not to Sir John Leslie or his agent, but to the Prior for the time being of the Island. In Muldoon's case it was paid by him in 1881 and up to the time of his death. Then it was paid by his successors in title until the time these proceedings were brought. Having settled that action Sir John Leslie's agent does nothing for the time being, and then because Muldoon wants some repairs done, which Sir John is willing to do, he enters into an agreement with him. That being so, I am going to submit in point of law that Muldoon was estopped on going back on the tenancy which he held from the Prior. I am going further to submit if he was not then estopped that in point of law the Agreement was fraudulently entered into and would be void. That being so, and if I succeed in establishing all these facts, this ejectment must fail. The evidence relied upon by Mr. Reid is that given by John Flood, who is now in occupation and possession

of the cabin in respect of which these proceedings were
brought. That being so, I don't see how these proceedings
can succeed, because one of the necessary parties has
not been served.

" Your Honour may naturally ask what is Archdeacon
Keown's position here to-day ? Is he here as a
beneficiary under the will or not ? I want to say at
once that at no time has Archdeacon Keown ever
exercised any benefit under the will of this lady or
claimed any benefit under it. His position as defendant
is in his capacity as Prior of the Island and legal custodian
duly authorised for the time being of the Roman Catholic
Bishop of the Diocese of Clogher, who claims to be the
owner of the Island. I will satisfy your Honour that
the Bishop in this case appointed the Prior. I am now
dealing with the particular cabin and want to make it
perfectly clear that we had not the smallest knowledge
of any Agreement or Letting by Sir John Leslie to Muldoon
until we got a copy of the Agreement through the courtesy
of the Plaintiff's solicitor when these proceedings were
started."

His Honour—" What is the legal position in regard
to tenants who pay two rents to two different landlords ?
It is an unusual thing in Ireland. The original title, I
think, holds good."

Mr. Lardner—" The earlier letting would probably
hold good whether it was right or wrong. We have been
receiving the rent long before 1884. Muldoon signed
the Agreement with Sir John Leslie to pay £1 0s. 0d. rent
per year for reasons best known to himself, and for such
inducements as were held out to him. That was done at a
time when the Bishop was in possession through the
Prior as his representative, and the Bishop claimed to be
possessed of the Island, and whether he was or not, the
present letting came under the terms of the Statute
and therefore this suit must fail. There was no rent paid
in respect of the Churches, the Hospices, or the Prior's
house, and the first attempt that was made to get rent
in respect of Muldoon's house was in 1884, after the action

of 1881. It was most significant that receipts for rent were produced only for years after 1881 when the action was settled. On that occasion the Plaintiffs claimed £200 damages for unlawfully entering the Plaintiffs' lands on Station Island and disturbing certain material there and in the Lake, and converting same to their own use, and also for an injunction to restrain the Defendant. There it is in the endorsement on the Writ. One is not inclined to put too much weight on the endorsement, but we find it amplified on the Plaintiffs' statement of claim.

" The Consent which was entered into is a most remarkable document (produced). That relates only to the portion of the Hospice which stood on the bed of the Lake. I will urge on your Honour in the strongest possible way that the meaning of that was that Sir John Leslie abandoned his claim in respect of the ownership of the soil of the Island. The action was brought in respect of the trespass on the bed of the Lake. The record was withdrawn and the action was settled on the lines that Defendant should acknowledge Sir John Leslie's ownership of the bed of the Lake and the soil of the Lake. I submit that that was an abandonment of any claim he had in respect of the Island, judging by the view taken up by Sir John and his predecessor when the Prior as agent for the Bishop always claimed that the ecclesiastical authorities were the owners of the Island. That has been their attitude, and it is their attitude still. The strongest fact in favour of the Defendant's case is that only three years after the action of 1881 this attempt was made to make a letting to Muldoon. The matter does not rest there because with the kindness and the readiness which I am glad to acknowledge, Sir John always gave a Lease when requested to do so, and we built a new Hospice there under a Lease given by Sir John at a nominal rent. He has always drawn a substantial rent from the person who works the Ferry. No rent has been charged in respect of the Churches, the Hospices or the Prior's house, and it is admitted that no rent has been charged in respect of the four cabins.

"I do not know what Sir John's contention really is, as we have acquired a title to the Island by reason of all these years of occupation. The occupants of the cabin accepted as their landlord the Prior for the time being and paid the rent to him at one penny per year, and later 1/- per year. The only evidence for the plaintiff was of some repairs to Muldoon's cabin, and they were not carried out at a time when the Prior was on the Island. I have no need to impress upon your Honour that in cases of this kind exercise of ownership must be under circumstances which are known and open. The Prior of the Island has made his case openly, and it certainly is consistent with the attitude which he has always taken up, consistent with the history of the Island, and consistent with the action brought in 1881, and the terms of the settlement. He never made any secret of his claim. The proceedings which took place between Muldoon and M'Grath do not affect us in the smallest way. I will prove that Archdeacon Keown, who was the representative of the Bishop, was not a party to these proceedings. Though Mrs. M'Grath went into occupation of the cabin, after Thomas Muldoon's death without the Prior's authority, yet the Prior accepted from her 1/- per year as rent. At the beginning of the subsequent season, the Prior refused to admit Mr. M'Grath into occupation of the cabin, and let it to Robert Muldoon, brother of the deceased, at 1/- per year as rent. That went on down to the time of Mary Muldoon's death, when Mr. Flood was put in her place.

"Originally these lands around Lough Derg were the property of Donogh M'Grath, who afterwards surrendered them to the Crown. There was an inquisition, as a result of which the transfer was compromised. Subsequently the lands passed to Dr. Spottiswoode, who was the Protestant Bishop of Clogher. The first time the lands came into possession of the Leslie family was through a Dr. John Leslie, whom one historian described as the 'Bishop of the Isles,' and who apparently not finding it either profitable or popular to be a Bishop in Scotland, came to Ireland and was appointed Protestant Bishop of Clogher, as a result of which he became possessed of these lands, which were valued at £3,500, at an annual rent of £60 and a fine of £400 per annum. Although the lands were then held by virtue of his office as Protestant Bishop of Clogher, the pilgrimage continued. Nothwithstanding the efforts made to discourage it, the pilgrimage continued to flourish as usual until at length the Government had an Act of Parliament passed forbidding people to frequent it, but this like all other similar attempts failed, and the pilgrimage went on, and is still going on. So far as the continuation of the pilgrimage is concerned, it is not denied, and its uninterrupted existence goes to support the claim now made on behalf of the Bishop in respect of the ownership of the Island.

" Originally the main seat—or what I may call the ecclesiastical establishment in Lough Derg—was Station Island, and at one time there was a monastery there. The monks afterwards lived on Saints' Island, which is indicated on the map. Every morning they crossed to Station Island and returned at night after the conclusion of the services of the day. In the course of events which followed, the monks were driven away from the monastery on Saints' Island, and the monastery was broken up.

" So far as the Bishop is concerned he is only anxious to do what is right and proper. In effect and in fact this is an attempt to claim the ownership of the whole Island, a claim which I respectfully submit should not have been made, especially by Sir John Leslie, when we bear in mind the result of the action in 1881. Your Honour will have no difficulty in coming to the conclusion that the case made on behalf of the defendant is a legal and consistent case."

Among those who gave evidence were : Archdeacon Patrick Keown, Enniskillen, who stated evidence that over £25,000 had been expended on the island by

the ecclesiastical authorities, and, since he took over
charge of it, he expended over £14,000. Mr. James
Riordan, solicitor, Dublin, produced a copy of the
Consent agreed to in 1881. Very Reverend Canon
Patrick Smyth, P.P., Clones, said that he was Prior
of Lough Derg from 1904 till 1909. During that time
the cabins or lodging-houses were all occupied by
tenants.

Mr. Reid (for Sir John Leslie) said : " Great stress has
been laid on the fact that we raised the point that Sir John
Leslie went to the island as owner, but there has been nothing
said in any shape or form about the building of Muldoon's
house in 1884 by us. The action in 1881 was settled, and
the case made here is that the Consent entered into with
them gave defendants the soil of the Island completely.
Not a word has been said about a thing which was
proved by several witnesses, and that was that in 1883
the Agent entered the Island in broad daylight with a
contractor, four other men, and George Crichton, and
partly pulled down the house which we now claim. That
was not done under any cloak of darkness, or at night.
Everybody could see what was going on, and while it
was going on the agent went out and fished in the Lake.
Surely if the Prior did not know of this at the time, he
learned it afterwards ? Why then didn't he assert his
title to the house ? He was bound to bring an action
at once and put Thomas Muldoon out of the house,
but instead of doing anything he allowed him to remain
in the house, and after his death his sister occupied the
house under her brother's will. Subsequently it went to
Robert Muldoon, and in 1909 Margaret M'Grath was in
possession of the house. It was only when the last of
the Muldoons died and the Prior took the house that it
was necessary for us to take action. There is no getting
away from the fact that a will was drawn up leaving the
house to Canon Keown, and it is a peculiar coincidence
that after the will was proved Canon Keown walked into
the house and took possession of it. Sir John Leslie
even made the road to the Lough. There is no-one who

knows him but would praise him for his liberality and generosity in every shape and form."

His Honour said : " I regret very much that it devolves upon me to give any decision in this case at all. The question involved in this case was ripe for decision thirty-five years ago, the parties then having employed very able and eminent Counsel on both sides, many of whom have now gone to the great majority. They had their evidence ready and they were near to a final determination of the question : yet at the last moment they shirked the proceedings, which were settled, not by the leaders in the case, but by the solicitors engaged, Mr. Riordan, who was examined before me, and Mr. Dane. I mention that, because to my mind it has a most important bearing on the evidence which was given before me yesterday and to-day. The bearing is this : in my view, reading the settlement of that action, and looking at the map which was made in connection with that settlement, it is perfectly clear that the late Sir John Leslie did not proceed to enforce his claim to the Island, so far as it was an island, but only to the bed and shores of the Lough, for by a most irregular line on the map the letting was made for ever of the shore, that is to say, the bed of the Lake on which the Hospice projected, and excluding the portion of the mainland of the Island on which the foundation of the Hospice stood. Well, it is perfectly manifest from that that it was intended to exclude the question of the ownership of the soil of the Island from the decision in that action. I can almost put it further and say that Sir John Leslie, then armed with a panoply of Counsel and so fortified, refused to proceed to assert his title. The bearing of that is this : both parties having made a settlement go back, and all the evidence given before me is conversant with events and matters that have occurred since that action was settled, and must take their complexion from efforts either side was making—I won't say to make evidence—but at all events with a view to a further case coming on. It is a most remarkable thing that the only agreement that can be produced by Sir John Leslie in regard to the letting of this lodging-house on the Island is a letting made in August, 1884, subsequent to that action to a man named Thomas Muldoon, a formal letting at £1 per year. The view I take— I may be wrong—is that that formal agreement was made with a view that possibly at a future time such as the present it would show that there was a definite agreement at a definite rent to Muldoon. It was continued from 1884 to the present time and the subject matter of these proceedings is the house that was then let to Thomas Muldoon. It is an action on ejectment brought by Sir John Leslie to recover possession of premises let in 1884 at £1 per year, and the rent for which has been paid to him for over thirty years. If stated in that way, it would appear that there was no answer to the action, and it could be further asserted that as between the tenants Muldoon and the present owner, M'Grath, there was litigation in this Court and I gave a decree against M'Grath, which was enforced and acted upon in an ejectment, and it appears strange that under these circumstances there should be a doubt about the right of the landlord of the surrounding estate to the house in question. You must throw yourself back, in my opinion into the state of affairs that existed in 1881 when the action was brought, and in my opinion you must really, if you may, try this question as matters then stood and not by the subsequent attempts by either party to make evidence at a later date. Of course it may be said, if you do that, what evidence have you to go upon ? Well, that is not the fault of the defendant. The title of Sir John Leslie is, I gather, as follows. I say " I gather " because no very tangible proof is given of it. We are asked to assume that the Leslie family have been there since 1660, and it may be assumed that in 1682 a Deed was made between the then Consistory and the Leslie family of the estates that surround Lough Derg. It is stated, and I believe it to be the case, that these lands were what was formerly called Church lands.

All these estates surrounding the Lough belonged to some Church prior to the Reformation, and there is no doubt that they belonged to what is known in this country as the Roman Catholic Church. That was so at the time the estates were confiscated and handed over to the Church of England. Then a certain Dr. Leslie, who was Bishop of the Isles, transferred his affections from Scotland to Donegal, and was put into possession of what was apparently the property of the Roman Catholic Church, the estates surrounding Lough Derg, and which were then in the possession of the Irish Protestant Church. That is, so far as I can gather from the history of it. You may ask what bearing that has on the case. The bearing is this : this ancient pilgrimage to St. Patrick's Purgatory has existed from time immemorial—I believe from the days of St. Patrick himself. We find it mentioned in the Annals of the Four Masters, and then there was a Statute in the reign of Queen Anne dealing with it, showing that it was in operation all through the ages, and the bearing it has to my mind is that it shows that when these estates were transferred, or changed possession from one Church to another in the course of the Reformation which has taken place in the history of this country, all through, the Roman Catholic Church, through its adherents, never gave up their possession in that sense that the Island was always used as a place of pilgrimage. The claim of Sir John Leslie arises from the fact that he owns the surrounding estate, which is in the possession of his tenants, and the inference is that the Island should pass to him. My view, having regard to the history of the place and the attempts that were made from time to time to prevent the use of the Island for the purpose of the pilgrimage, is that it is only a natural inference that the Church held on to it through the ages, and that possession of it never really passed in one sense along with the rest of the estate. If you come to examine the class of Island it is, it is a barren rock that owes its entire historical importance and everything else to the fact of the glamour thrown around it, as it is alleged to be a place where St. Patrick once lived and where the pilgrims and devotees went to make their pilgrimage. Otherwise it is valuable to nobody, and it is only an example of the devotion of the Church. Buildings have been erected on it, and can it be said for a moment that these buildings could now be recovered by the Leslie family under an ejectment ? Certainly not. I am sure that nothing could be further from their views, and nothing in my opinion could be further from their legal title, because no rent has been paid to them. Apparently many of the buildings have been erected without their consent. In regard to the recent hospice, there is a lease for ever, but it is only applicable to the bed of the lake and not to the confines of the Island. Every one of the buildings was a tacit admission that Sir John Leslie was not claiming rent or right in respect of the main ground of the Island which was uncovered with water. It is said, of course, that it is all very well to speak of the settlement in connection with the Island, but there is no doubt that the actual rights have grown up. From one cause or another these lodging houses on the Island have been a valuable source of income to the persons who occupied them, and who were from the mainland. Of course they are from the mainland. Nobody ever thought of living permanently on the Island and nobody ever does. If the tenants are from the mainland they must be from Sir John Leslie's tenantry, because the land all round the Island consists of his property. It is an extraordinary fact if the Island belonged to the Leslie family that they never got any rent from the tenants of the cabins, except from Muldoon, and that was under a lease made subsequent to the action of 1881. Then it is alleged that there is a cottage or waiting-house in connection with the ferry. At first I thought it was a ferry house, but it is not. It is a lodging-house, but the person who works the ferry has been in occupation of it. It has nothing to do with the facilities of working the ferry, and the mention of ferryhouse was only made subsequent to the action of 1881. None of the other lodging-house keepers ever paid any rent directly to Sir John Leslie, and you find that all of them contemporaneously, with the addition of Muldoon, who also paid £1 per year to Sir John Leslie, all of them acknowledged the dominion of the Prior and paid him in the early times a penny per year, or a shilling per year at a later date. That all goes to show that the religious community, controlled by the Prior, under the direction of the Bishop of Clogher, exercised dominion over the Island, which is only natural, having regard to the ancient history in connection with the Church. I think it is unfortunate that these proceedings have not been taken seriously before a Superior Court. It is intimated to me that no matter what way I decide the matter will eventually find its way back to Lifford, and I am very pleased at that. I had hoped that the opportunity for thought afforded by adjourning the case overnight might have resulted in some amicable settlement of the case. It is to be regretted that the harmonious relations alleged to have existed for such a long time should not be made perpetual. I think there is a very simple way of doing it, because the temporal interest in this house is a very trifling matter, only £1 0s. 0d. per year, and no other house has been suggested. There is undoubtedly a large interest in what is called the ferry. That interest seems to have grown up entirely through the fact of the prosperity, if I may use the term, of the Station. It entirely depends upon the progress of the Church. In 1839 the rent of this ferry was £240 0s. 0d. a year. Some years ago it was £50, and now it is £80. It is a valuable right, and it seems to me that it depends upon the prosperity of the religious community, and if importance is attached to it, it is to the interest of Sir John Leslie, and it should calculate to make a friendly feeling between the parties. That is the reason I put it to the parties between themselves that they should carefully consider the matter. I would have thought that as there is some acknowledgment to Sir John Leslie's right to the ferry that he might very readily have abandoned his claim to this small house. The pilgrimage to St. Patrick's Purgatory has been going on for years, and in my opinion the original Church to which the Island belonged has never laid aside its claim. It never offered or consented to acknowledge that anybody else could have dominion entirely over this ancient and holy ground. Accordingly, I say I am not satisfied with the evidence for the plaintiff, and I dismiss the case."

An appeal was made against the dismissal. The case was again listed for hearing at the Summer Assizes, Lifford, the following July. The pilgrimage season was then in full swing and there was a large number on the island when the Prior was preparing to leave for Lifford in order again to give evidence. Once more he told the pilgrims the whole story and asked them to organize a special watch before the Blessed Sacrament until the hearing of the case was concluded.

There ensued at the Lifford Courthouse a very curious repetition of history. It was again the 16th July and all parties were assembled in court to hear the case, when plaintiff's solicitor approached defendants' counsel with a suggested settlement, exactly as had happened thirty-six years previously.

A Consent was later signed by Sir John Leslie, Bart., Most Rev. Dr. M'Kenna, Bishop of Clogher, Archdeacon Keown, Mr. James Dunleavy, solicitor, and Mr. Reid, solicitor, reading as follows :—

" It is hereby consented and agreed :

(1) That the Ferry rights be conveyed absolutely to three trustees to be named by the Catholic Bishop of Clogher.

(2) That a road twenty feet wide ending at the boundary of the acre on the mainland be vested in the County Council of Donegal by Plaintiff, and pending such vesting Plaintiff shall keep same in reasonable repair.

(3) That the Ferry shall be confined to the nearest reasonable route to Station Island from the landing-stage at the mainland and on return.

(4) That one acre of land on the mainland be conveyed to the said trustees, with twenty-five feet of the bed of the Lake opposite thereto to hold in fee simple.

(5) That turbary be conveyed to the said trustees.

(5a) In addition to the acre of the bed of Lough Derg in the next clause mentioned a strip twenty-five feet wide of the Lake bed is to be vested in the said trustees from the Ladies' Hospice to a line drawn from the south-east end of St. Mary's Chapel to meet the shore. No buildings to be erected on this last-mentioned strip.

(6) That one acre of the Lake bottom from the south-east end of the existing land slips toward the west side of the land be conveyed to the trustees to hold in fee simple.

(6a) The Plaintiff and the trustees of the Plaintiff's estate shall, if required, convey any estate right, title or claim he or they may have to Station Island to the aforesaid trustees absolutely in fee.

(7) That all existing leases and grants or easements be confirmed and converted into perpetual grants free of rent.

(8) That no houses, save waiting-rooms or buildings necessary for the proper working of the Ferry and Car Service, be erected on the mainland. The Plaintiff is to supply stone for building same at half the price heretofore charged, and stone at the present price to be given for building on Station Island from Ballymaca-vanny quarry, so long as such is there procurable. The said trustees shall pay £2,000 to the Plaintiff or the trustees of the Plaintiff's estate for the premises. No steamboat shall

> be used for ferrying or otherwise. Any question
> in dispute shall be decided by Mr. D. S.
> Henry, K.C., and Mr. W. E. Wylie, K.C."

The Consent was handed in.

Certain Catholic friends and advisers objected to
such a large sum being paid for the freedom of the
pilgrimage, but time has proved the Agreement to be a
wise one. When news of the settlement reached the
island, one of the women pilgrims exclaimed : " I am
proud to be here on Independence Day ! "

Since that time, a great part of the Leslie estate,
including most of the land around Lough Derg, has
passed into the hands of the Irish Land Commission.
In July 1941, the Forestry Department wrote to the
Prior reminding him that he was cutting and taking away
turf without authority from their Forestry land, and
saying that he could have the use of a bank selected
by their representative, on payment of 7s. a year.
Monsignor Keown admitted the accusation, but pointed
out that the Prior of Lough Derg had cut turf from time
immemorial free of all charge and that this prescription
was confirmed after the litigation of 1917 in Deed by Sir
John Leslie, the privilege being granted not only to the
pilgrimage authorities but to all the people who are
permanently employed by them in connection with the
pilgrimage. On reading the Deed the Department withdrew their objection and apologised for any incon-
venience caused. The right of free turbary was thus
established for all time and the last link broken in the
chain that had been forged around Lough Derg for a
thousand years.

There was in later years a pleasant sequel to all that
legal contention. When the present Basilica was consecrated, the late Sir John Leslie presented it with a painting of the Madonna by Murillo, bearing the inscription :

Donum Familiae Leslie de Glass Lough
Ecclesiae S. Patricii apud Lough Derg, 1929.

To the donor's disappointment, the painting was not hung in the church. Both Sir John Lavery, whose opinion was sought, and the architect were firm in their opinion that no picture should be hung there, as it would conflict with the austere design and planned simplicity of that interior. The painting was therefore hung in the outer sacristy.

The late Sir John Leslie's eldest son, now Sir Shane Leslie, became in early life a convert to the Catholic Church. He has written several books on Lough Derg, including a large compilation of documents bearing on the history of the island and its place in literature, testimony to great patience and erudition. His book is indispensable to the student and historian.

In conclusion, a very different atmosphere now invests the relationship between the pilgrimage and the family that once exercised dominion over the lake. Favoured visitors to the Leslies' home, Glaslough, are—with the Prior's willing consent—taken to Station Island to view the buildings. The tour of inspection naturally includes a visit to the Acolytes' Sacristy in the Basilica, where the Murillo may be admired.

IX. RESURGENCE

EARLY in the twentieth century, it became clear that, even with the new hospice, the accommodation on Station Island was still far from adequate. It was decided in 1909 to devote the existing hospice to men only and to build an entirely new one for women. This work was set in hands and a second extensive guesthouse, capable of accommodating three hundred, was opened for women in 1912. Most of the foundations of this building rest on the bed of the lake. The different floors are partitioned and curtained off into several hundred cubicles, each cubicle fitted with a modern spring bed and all necessary toilet requisites. A little detail that causes most pilgrims a great deal of surprise is that the beds are furnished with real linen, not cotton, sheets, and pure woollen blankets.

The relief of having at last secured ample housing accommodation was marred during the very year this new hospice opened by a very serious outbreak of typhoid fever among the pilgrims. There had been slight outbreaks of this trouble during a number of successive years. Although it had been the recommended practice there to drink no water which had not been boiled, some pilgrims persisted in drinking water taken directly out of the lake. This water was analysed and condemned because it was polluted by sewerage. The Donegal Board of Health took up the matter. They gave their opinion that the pilgrimage would have to be closed down altogether unless a pure water supply, other than that from the lake, could be immediately provided for the pilgrims.

The Prior now had to turn his attention to this pressing problem. All the surrounding land was examined for the purpose and it was found that the nearest source of safe water was in Lake Carricknamaddy, in the mountains to the south-west, nearly two miles from the island.

It was a very big and expensive engineering job to convey this water by pipeline down the mountain and along the bottom of the lake bed direct to the island. However, a loan was raised and the work begun. The required line of piping was about 2,600 yards long, the greater part of it running down the mountain side and the remainder resting on the lake bottom. The contractor defaulted in the middle of the work and other troubles arose before it was completed. Nevertheless, the 1914 season found this pure water available on tap in the island. From that date, fever among the pilgrims was never heard of again.

The year 1913 was memorable for Cardinal Logue's visit. He spent a whole day on the Island and watched the pilgrims going through their exercises. In his reply to the address of welcome presented to him, the cardinal in his own inimitable way proclaimed the pilgrimage as a very special help in attaining salvation :—

"When I was a young priest, I often had occasion to attend at their deathbeds numbers of people who made the pilgrimage to Lough Derg, and every one of these deathbeds was the deathbed of a saint. There was no need to get them to make general confessions or to repair anything in their past lives. One visit to Lough Derg was enough to secure that, and some of those I attended were in the habit of coming here every year. I gave them, of course, the Sacraments of the Church, and especially the greatest of all the Sacraments to strengthen them on their journey to eternity, but I often thought that if they had died in the deserts of Central Africa they were sure to go to Heaven. They owed that to the instruction they received, the penance they performed, and the exercises of piety which they went through in this holy place. Hence I have been highly edified on my visit to this holy island to find the people here in such numbers . . . . The pilgrimage has been a great grace to thousands and thousands ;

it has been the beginning of sanctification for thousands upon thousands. I have no doubt that whatever else changes in Ireland, Lough Derg will never change. It is as unchangeable as the hills by which we are surrounded. So long as the Irish Church exists it will be a home of penance, and piety, and sanctification, and a source of wonderful graces to those who come here to make the Stations. Missions and retreats are now very general throughout the country; and they are doing great good among the people; but, somehow, none of them gives the same spiritual mouthful as Lough Derg gives. I often intended to come here and do some little thing to make up for my unruly life—but when the time came there was always some new duty to be discharged that made me put it off; but I hope before I die to be able to carry it out still. . . . . I believe any person who goes through the routine here on Lough Derg, the penitential exercises, the fasting, and the prayers to which so many Indulgences are granted—I believe if he died after leaving it, he would have very little to suffer in the next world . . . . When you pass out, greater crowds will come here during the next two months, and they will find what you have found, and what tens of thousands of other Catholics have found here : they will find here that peace which surpasses all understanding, peace with God, peace with their neighbours, and peace with themselves. This is a regular haven of peace. It would be impossible for a man to come in here with rancour in his mind. If he had any little touch of it it drops into the lake either on his way in, or on his way out of the Island."

Cardinal Logue referred to the special indulgences that may be gained at Lough Derg. These are: a plenary indulgence, applicable to the souls in Purgatory, by each pilgrim who complies with the usual conditions. Again, there is a picture hanging in St. Mary's Church which has been certified an authentic copy of the miraculous picture of Our Lady of Perpetual Succour, now preserved in the Church of St. Alphonsus, Rome. This picture was specially blessed by Pope Pius X for Lough Derg, and the following indulgences attached to it : (1) a plenary indulgence on the anniversary day of its erection, that is, the 13th August, for ever, to each pilgrim who prays before the picture and complies with the usual conditions ; (2) three hundred days to be gained once a day by each pilgrim who visits the picture and there prays for the Holy Father's intentions. An indulgence of one hundred days, to be gained once a day, is also attached to the prayer to Our Lady of Perpetual Succour. There is a special Mass of St. Patrick celebrated every morning in St. Patrick's Church during the pilgrimage season.

Occasional freakish summer storms are peculiar to Lough Derg. Pilgrims alighting at the shore on a tranquil summer day are often surprised at the unexpected commotion of the deeps and the dark yeasty appearance of the water. The pilgrimage season of 1918 was long remembered for its storms. On Sunday, June 9th, pilgrims arriving on the shore were confronted with an awesome spectacle, the lake being like a boiling cauldron of spouting water. Although the transit to Station Island takes only ten minutes in normal conditions, there was not even this interval of calm all that day from nine o'clock in the morning until eight in the evening. The lake shore was packed with waiting pilgrims, most of them fasting. On the following Thursday, June 13th, a storm broke over the lake again. The large boat, the " St. Patrick," left the mainland for Station Island during the morning with thirty-one pilgrims, of whom seventeen were women. The Prior steered the boat. The storm rapidly increased in violence and the boat was compelled to put in for shelter behind Rough Island. A smaller boat then went over and the Prior and a few men

returned. Later the marooned passengers were divided
up between lighter craft in the hope that the small boats
would make headway against the wind and waves.
Even this plan did not work. The smaller boats made
several ineffective attempts to get across to the Island.
In the end, all were obliged to return to the mainland
and wait in the ferry house until the storm subsided.
The pilgrims did not land on Station Island until eleven
o'clock that night.

Fourteen years passed before there is mention in the
records of another such violent upheaval of the waters.
Hundreds of pilgrims were kept waiting on the mainland
the whole day on the 6th August, 1932. The largest
boat on the ferry, the " St. Patrick," could not be
launched at all that day, but the next largest, the " St.
Columba," succeeded in crossing four times in the late
afternoon. Five days later, in the evening, when all the
pilgrims were landed, another furious storm broke out
this time with a fantastic display of lightning which
continued for nearly two hours, and a deafening barrage
of thunder, reverberating through the mountains.

The great majority of those who make the pilgrimage
to Lough Derg are Irish. A large number of exiled Irish,
notably from Liverpool and Glasgow, are also faithful.
Although many of those pilgrims may be three
generations removed from the homeland, they are dogged
in their loyalty to St. Patrick's Purgatory. In the back
streets and slum areas of many an English and Scottish
city, the name of Lough Derg evokes nostalgic memories.
Young people are inspired by their elders with a burning
desire to perform this devotion so peculiarly Irish ;
it is in their blood ; for the same reason, Irish-Americans
and Australians are also frequent among the pilgrims.

The number of English pilgrims, on the other hand,
is small and they are drawn from the aristocracy and
intelligentsia. Once in recent years the secretary of
the Catholic Truth Society of England wrote to the

Prior of Lough Derg to make arrangements for an English pilgrimage of five hundred people. In the ensuing correspondence the Prior indicated that it might be difficult to house five hundred at one time together with the usual Irish contingents. The final arrangement made was that two hundred and fifty were to come one week and two hundred and fifty at a later date. But when the pilgrimage came to be organized the whole thing fell through, apparently through lack of enthusiasm. The secretary wrote at a later date to the Prior that the proposed pilgrimage " will be represented by one gentleman."

This incident merely goes to show how peculiarly Irish is the Lough Derg devotion. Many a pilgrim who goes to the Island for the first time remarks that the most surprising feature of the place is its obscure familiarity. He finds that he cannot shake off the feeling that he has already seen it all, experienced it all. As he plods over the rough stones in bare feet this sense of a warm and friendly intimacy returns with renewed conviction. There is a satisfaction in that fast unrivalled by the most epicurean meal in memory. The very strangeness of the whole rite is like an old memory overlaid by time.

Most pilgrims develop for this rocky island and its harsh routine an affection that really defies explanation. Again and again they return to it with a gaiety, an uplifting of the heart, a profound sense of relief, in short the very sentiments proper to homecoming after lifelong exile. That which speaks to them at Lough Derg is *race*. In going there they are answering the call of blood.

During that disturbed period of Irish history called " the Trouble " strange instances occurred of the deep affinity between this particular devotion and the Irish people. There were two hundred and sixty-four interned political prisoners at Ballykinlar in County Down who got the idea of doing the pilgrimage in their camp. It was not their chaplain who suggested this to them.

They were not all ex-pilgrims to the island. The majority
of them had never even heard of Lough Derg. A few
among them had made the pilgrimage and they told
the others about it. Soon most of the prisoners expressed
a wish to join in. Their chaplain consulted the Prior and
was told that the plan was feasible under the extraordinary
circumstances. Next, the men asked permission from the
prison Governor. He was surprised, but he agreed to
everything except the all-night vigil. A fourth station
was therefore substituted each day to make up for this
omission. From the 11th to the 15th August, 1921, these
men faithfully performed the devotions as if actually on
the pilgrimage, including the strict fast. This was probably
the first time in history that the rite was carried out at
such a distance from island and lake. Every detail
of this peculiar act of faith was later given by one of
the interned " pilgrims " in a letter to the Prior. He
had a special medal struck to commemorate the event
and sent one to each of the men who took part.

The year 1922 is remembered in the modern history
of Lough Derg for a most agitated pilgrimage season.
The disturbances shaking Ireland that year naturally had
repercussions also on the island. When the Prior and
attendants crossed to the shrine a week before the season
opened, as is the custom, in order to prepare for the
arrivals, the whole district was given up to guerilla
warfare between British and Irish. Skirmishes between
the Ulster Specials and the Republicans were an everyday occurrence. Pettigo, the island postal town, was
a storm centre, because it happens to be also a border
town. Telephone and telegraph wires were cut there
and the Post Office was closed for a long time. (This
little town, chief gateway to the pilgrimage, has since
become one of the tragic jokes of Partition. It is divided
by the river Tarmon and . . . by the Border. The population of a few hundred enjoy the dubious advantages of
two Post Offices, one Irish, one British ; two Customs
Offices, two police stations, each under a different
Government, and the same kind of duplication of all

other urban administrative services !) Trains were held up on several occasions. About twenty passengers on their way to Lough Derg were made go back to Enniskillen and remain there for a week-end. Finally, the train service on the Bundoran line was suspended for three weeks. No hackney cars would venture out.

Despite such deterrent conditions, a small number of pilgrims continued to arrive daily at the island. The Prior of the period was the only Confessor doing duty that whole season.

On June 4th British military marched into Pettigo with heavy field guns and other equipment. The small band of irregular soldiers holding the town surrendered and were given fifteen minutes to leave. The British then took complete control of Pettigo. Strict curfew was enforced every day from 2 p.m. in the afternoon until 10 a.m. the following morning, and a permit was required for passing through the town even between 10 a.m. and 2 p.m.

The adventures of a group of five women pilgrims were typical of the times. Two of these were from Dublin, two from Cavan, and one from Sligo. The Prior applied to the Commander at Pettigo for permission for these pilgrims to pass through that town on their way back to their various destinations. He received no answer. The women eventually left the island, taking a north-eastern direction for their southern destinations. They were rowed across the lake to that part of the shore where county Tyrone abuts on it. They passed through Castlederg to touch the Derry railway line at Victoria Bridge, where they got a train to Enniskillen. One has to look at a map to appreciate the circular tour forced on these pilgrims by the fortunes of war.

Lough Derg was completely isolated from the post for three weeks. At length letters were conveyed from the northern end of the lake to Donegal. They were thereafter carried three times a week by motor from Donegal to the end of the mountain road, thence by special messenger to the lake shore near the mouth of the

Fluchlyn river where a boat was in readiness to take them to Station Island.

After about three weeks' suspension of service the Bundoran railway line again re-opened. A car timidly appeared to convey passengers to the lake shore. This vehicle was followed by others. By the middle of August there were seven or eight side-cars, one motor and one lorry on the road. Halfway through the season, there was a welcome relaxation of the curfew in Pettigo. By the time the pilgrims dispersed, conditions were almost normal again.

During the whole period that martial law was enforced in Pettigo, pilgrims continued to arrive at Station Island by a route diametrically opposite to the usual one. They crossed the Donegal hills and landed at the island on the side farthest away from Pettigo. A sympathetic look-out was maintained from the island towards that northern shore. Whenever a group of pilgrims was sighted, a boat was immediately sent across for them.

The ancient right of sanctuary for fugitives was claimed on the island during this memorable season of disturbance. One night twenty Republican soldiers crossed over from the Donegal hills looking for refuge. The Prior was in a sore predicament. If the men were traced to the sanctuary it would certainly be raided, with inevitable destruction and bloodshed, as feeling just then was running very high. Such an occurrence would be bound to end the pilgrimage that year, if not for several years. On the other hand, he knew all the men : they were farmers' sons from the district ; he could not deny them his sympathy. He talked it out with them and, when they realized that their presence might seriously endanger the lives of the pilgrims, they decided to move off again. After rest and a meal they prepared to leave, still cheerful and friendly. They knelt for the Prior's blessing and promised, if their lives were spared, to return and make the pilgrimage. They kept this promise to a man.

Despite the perils and hardships of travel in the 1922

season 1,308 people made the pilgrimage. The figures for the previous year, however, were 8,324 and, for 1923, 6,000. It will be understood, then, that when the Prior balanced his books at the end of the 1922 season he found himself burdened with a catering loss of no less than £1,000.

The curious demonstration of love for Lough Derg on the part of the Ballykinlar prisoners found an echo two years later in another internment prison. During August, 1923, two hundred and sixty-six prisoners were cooped up on board the prison ship *Argenta*, anchored in Belfast Lough. One hundred and ninety-four, or more than two-thirds of their number, banded together to make the Lough Derg pilgrimage. The circumstances were identical with Ballykinlar inasmuch as most of the men knew nothing about the Lough Derg pilgrimage until they heard about it in the prison. In this case, four of the prisoners were forced to give up through physical weakness. The devotions ended on the 10th August. A description of this version of the " pilgrimage " is preserved in a letter to the Prior from the chaplain for the time being of the *Argenta*. The " pilgrims " in this case were all decent men, who served their country according to their convictions. On board the prison ship they were treated as miscreants. The pilgrimage can hardly ever have been performed under circumstances of greater pathos. On this occasion, too, a special medal was struck as a token of remembrance.

Transport problems connected with the pilgrimage had always been a matter of concern to those in charge of the island. An effort was made for the first time in the year 1912 to get the railway companies (there were eight of them in Ireland at that period) to give special concessions to travellers to Lough Derg, who comprised thousands of their passengers every summer. Concessions had indeed been given by the railway companies, but in a reluctant and indefinite way. Very often, even after the concessions had been granted by the company managements, individual booking clerks in different parts

of the country persistently refused to accord them.
In such cases, the Prior felt obliged to make a refund.
However, now that the annual number of travellers to
Lough Derg begins to steady around the figure of 15,000,
the railway companies have at last realised the importance
of the pilgrimage and one may get a return ticket to
Pettigo from any part of Ireland at a special cheap rate.

But the railway stops at Pettigo, four miles south
of the lake. The remainder of the journey was usually
done in horse-drawn vehicles, such as traps, wagonettes,
or sidecars, until motors became frequent. Motors and
lorries, driven by private individuals, then replaced
the older type of vehicle. It proved a great deal more
difficult to bring those drivers under control than it
had been to wring concessions from the railway companies.
The car-drivers were truculent ; they both overcharged
the pilgrims and treated them unfairly. There was fierce
competition among the drivers, in the excitement of
which the pilgrims' comfort and convenience were
completely ignored. The cars and lorries (pilgrims having
to stand in these latter) were grossly over-crowded ;
they speeded in a most terrifying and dangerous way.
Those vehicles, racing to and fro every day during the
season, all but collided at corners and the threat of a
dire accident was perpetually present. Sometimes returning pilgrims were hustled out on to the roadside
within a mile, or even two miles, of their destination
and rudely told to walk the rest of the way. The car
then doubled back in a mad race for another complement
of passengers. When it was a question of catching a
train at Pettigo, the pilgrims, who were fasting and weary,
were forced to run a mile or so, burdened with their
luggage. Their plight can be imagined. Again, a great
number of the cars in use were antiquated and in bad
repair. During the 1925 season a lorry broke down on
the return journey holding up a line of other vehicles,
with the result that sixty passengers missed the midday train at Pettigo. This made it impossible for most
of those passengers to reach their homes that night.

During every pilgrimage season for years and years, a tide of complaints used to reach the Prior from all parts of Ireland, written in indignation as soon as the pilgrims got home. His verbal remonstrances with the car-drivers proved quite useless.

Before the 1926 season opened, the Prior caused a circular to be printed and sent to all the car-owners engaged in the Pettigo—Lough Derg service, demanding an undertaking not to overcrowd the passengers. He complained strongly of the discomforts and dangers to which passengers were exposed, the usual practice being to crush nine passengers into an ordinary motor-car, and twenty-six into a lorry. This printed remonstrance had no better effect than the verbal protests.

As the hackney-drivers persisted in their high-handed methods, arrangements were at last made, in 1929, with the Great Northern Railway Company for a fleet of 'buses to take over the transport of pilgrims from Pettigo to the lake shore. This step caused quite a storm of local dissatisfaction and criticism. The car-drivers, who were thus deprived of their means of liveli-hood, were an object of sympathy entirely undeserved in view of the facts. Early that year, when the new arrangements became known, the Donegal County Council took up the car-drivers' case. The lake-going road had been vested in the County Council since the 1917 settlement. A motion on behalf of the car-drivers was tabled to the effect that only motors and light lorries be allowed the use of the Pettigo—Lough Derg road. On a vigorous protest from the Prior and a full explana-tion, the resolution was wisely dropped.

The deterrent effect of these drivers' conduct on would-be pilgrims, who were sensitive and timid, is something that can never be calculated. The struggle with them, therefore, was from many points of view, the hardest test the pilgrimage had had to endure. The pilgrim's journey from the remotest corner of Ireland to Station Island has now been properly organised : the railway companies have been induced to do their part ; transport has been regulated between Pettigo and the lake shore. The final stage of the journey, over that mile of water separating mainland from island, was the easiest to order as the ferrymen were always more or less under the direct control of the pilgrimage.

The mode of conveying pilgrims to and fro on the water has never been modernised. Large row-boats are used for the purpose to-day, as they have been used from time immemorial. They are clumsy-looking craft, built for safety rather than for elegance. They are unique in their dimensions and, so far as is known, are the biggest row-boats in the world. The largest one can accommodate one hundred and fifty passengers. They are propelled by four very large oars, each oar plied by three or four men, who stand at the job. These boats are constructed on the lake shore by a skilled boat-maker from Killybegs. Each boat is christened after an Irish saint, with traditional ceremony and with the blessing prescribed in the Ritual, and the pilgrim finds himself being borne across in the direct care of " Saint Patrick," " Saint Brigid," " Saint Columba," or " Saint Macarten." The boats are examined and tested every year by an expert, and pronounced sea-worthy before the new season opens.

In former times the ferry used to be rented each year by a family who paid a variable rent for it to the landlord. This rent was fixed in recent times at £50 a year. There was a time in the middle of the nineteenth century when the ferry rental was worth about £300 a year to the landlord. The ferryman easily earned this rent and made a profit from the tariff charged to pilgrims. Writers hostile to the pilgrimage used to make scornful reference to this toll exacted by the Protestant proprietor for what Sir Shane Leslie calls " his Charon-like right of ferry."

The only instance in history when the ferry gave serious trouble to the ecclesiastical authorities was early in the nineteenth century when a Protestant boatman had the monopoly. This man tried to increase his

legitimate profits in two objectionable ways : he consented to take anyone at all who applied to him across
to the island, regardless of the Prior's ruling that no
visitors were to be admitted during the pilgrimage season
without special permission.   Secondly, he instituted
dances, or " patterns," on the lake shore during the
season, functions that sometimes turned into drunken
orgies. This abuse became so serious that the pilgrimage
had to be closed down for a year, in 1829, until the abuse
had been stamped out. As we have seen, the diocese of
Clogher purchased the ferry rights at the conclusion of
the 1917 litigation. The ferryman and boatmen are
now in the service of the Church, adequately paid for
their services, and contented.

Pilgrims of the mid-twentieth century can hardly
realize the different conditions under which they can
now make this devotion. The quiet person, intent only
on saying his prayers, who undertakes the Lough Derg
pilgrimage to-day can with difficulty imagine the amount
of organisation and labour that have been continuously
expended to preserve for him that very quietude which
he takes for granted. He can now make his journey at
a moderate cost and under reasonable conditions of
comfort, unharrassed by buccaneering profit-makers. His
privacy while on the island is assured. He is adequately
accommodated.   All risk of incidental sickness and
hardship has been removed. With a world at war those
qualities of simplicity and quietude, which give this
place its special prestige, have acquired a value beyond
expression.   They are the only balm for the world's
annealing. Amidst the chaos made by civilisations
thundering down, the preservation of this penitential
discipline seems an achievement little short of miraculous.

X. THE BASILICA

An Irishman going to Lough Derg to-day is surprised to find what he might least expect, so uncommon is it still in Ireland : majesty of building. Knowing the general poverty of architecture in this country, he will probably go there for the first time without high hopes, resigned to finding the usual inadequate compromise, sham Gothic out of the much-worn pattern book, or its modern successor, the cheap concrete structure, tricked out with meretricious decoration and distressing statuary. Instead, he is confronted with the Basilica of Saint Patrick, a building which so nobly fulfils its purpose that to see such completion even once in a lifetime is to count oneself blessed.

The achievement is all the more remarkable because the finished structure is the product of two architects in succession, an arrangement usually considered detrimental to unity. Professor W. A. Scott designed this church in 1919. He was a man of unusual genius, who was chiefly responsible for developing a native Irish style of architecture. But for his untimely death before he reached his full powers, he might have carried this style to a high degree of perfection and to international fame. Scott was in some sort the favourite, if not the discovery, of the Clogher diocese, where he got every scope to develop his talent. He first acquired distinction with a plan he submitted, in open competition, for a new Town Hall in Enniskillen. Previous to this, he had been employed by the London County Council and he was at the time completely unknown in Ireland. His plan for the Enniskillen Town Hall so far outrivalled those submitted by the other competitors that he won the commission. Asked whether he could make certain fundamental changes in the plan and return it quickly to the judges, Scott promised to have it ready next morning. He stayed up all night at the work and kept his promise. To Scott is owed, at least partially, the success of Loughrea Cathedral; the lovely Church at Spiddal, Galway; the O'Growney Mausoleum in Maynooth; the Chapel in the Convent of Mercy, Enniskillen; the Celtic Cross in Lourdes presented by the Irish Pilgrimage in 1913, and many other works.

As Scott's talent developed, he proved also to have more than his share of the erratic waywardness commonly associated with genius. When asked to prepare a plan for a new large church on Station Island, he came there and spent a night on the island observing the pilgrimage and its setting. Early next morning, he was seen leaving in a boat. The Prior thought he had completed his preliminary view and was going away. But no; Scott got the man to row him a certain distance from the island to a point where he considered he had a comprehensive view. Here he thought deeply for a little while, returned, and announced that he had the plan already made. He died two years after he had furnished the design for this church, no progress meanwhile having been made with the building, as the political upheavals made such enterprise out of the question. The foundation stone of St. Patrick's was not laid until 1926, and Professor Scott's design had then to be put into the hands of another architect, Mr. T. J. Cullen, who carried out the plans.

The excellence of this building is that it has seized the essential idea and spirit of St. Patrick's Purgatory and petrified it in a fashion worthy of its ancient prestige and its historical associations. That ethos is penance. Despite the soaring fantasies of the Knight Owen and his followers, or the embellishments of literary fancy, the whole significance of the Purgatory is penance.

The church that conveys this idea is plain and massive in design, eschewing what is merely elegant or ornate. Its form is octagonal: the unusual pointed roof of steel, composed of six layers of material, beginning with wood and ending with copper, is also octagonal, the whole giving an impression of great strength. The style is that which has now come to be described as "Hiberno-Romanesque," as it is a development of the Irish Romanesque, which began with Cormac's chapel at Cashel, exhibiting the rounded arches that are such a conspicuous feature of all early Irish work, and which predominate in Scott's church also.

The bold, plain outline of St. Patrick's Basilica harmonizes with the empty and solemn landscape of lake and mountain in which it stands. Its massive, grey walls, surmounted by a pointed dome of that peculiar greenish hue assumed by weathered copper, take the shape of an enormous lantern : a good symbol, for St. Patrick's Purgatory has been like a lantern shedding light not only over Ireland, but formerly over all Europe.

It is built solidly of stone from a local quarry, a good stone with the peculiarity that it cannot be dressed. The architraves, string-courses and all the dressed stones in the building are therefore taken from the famous Carrickmacross limestone quarry, that yields a stone which dresses perfectly. The church is doubly built, as the inside walls are lined with blocks of reinforced concrete for greater solidity.

In keeping with the principle that it commemorates, austerity is its keynote. The huge strength of the exterior is re-echoed in the deliberate simplicity of the interior, an effect most carefully calculated. The lines within have not been broken by the confusion of a single curtain, or drapery, or pictures, or even flowers on the altar. But it is a cheerful and happy austerity, for the skilful lighting dissipates the least suggestion of gloom. It has been difficult and it will always be difficult, to preserve that austerity so deeply satisfying. One can but pray that the successive Priors of the pilgrimage will be always strong-minded. The donors of shrines, those ubiquitous monied persons with devotion and no judgment, will be busy here too : they will seek to intrude in this church as everywhere else, longing to spoil the fresh miracle of its interior with their wearisome disorder of pious fripperies.

Photographs do very scant justice to St. Patrick's for a special reason. At each side of the entrance, there is a loggia (or porch) approached by a flight of broad, shallow steps. Holy Mass may be celebrated in those porches. Since photographers are not allowed on the island during the pilgrimage season, these loggias are shown empty in photographs, whereas they are an architectural feature really made for crowds. Vacant, they are meaningless, but the whole building seems to spring to life when human figures appear under the arches. No pilgrim to Lough Derg has ever seen those loggias bereft of human figures, and that is why the photographs have such an air of unfamiliarity. The porches are possessed by people all through the season : groups standing, sitting, strolling, from dawn to dusk, and throughout the night too, when crowds leave the church at intervals between the Stations.

This is a place to which a man comes in order to confront the reality of himself. The church presiding over this soul-searching could not contain anything pretentious or sham without a serious affront to good taste. There is here, therefore, no wood painted to look like marble ; no cement pretending to be stone ; no tin lacquered to look like bronze. The core of the deep satisfaction in St. Patrick's Church is its absolute genuineness.

The sanctuary walls and floor are lined with marble of rare beauty. The panels at the back of the high altar, the side altars and their supporting pillars are a dove grey, while around the sanctuary are marble panels, whose prevailing hue is old gold, inset into surrounds of white. The variegation in the veining of this marble is so unusual that it is fascinating. The three altars, Communion rails and pulpit are of marble also in delicately blended tints. Two white marble statues stand out against the grey and gold and rich traceries : St. Dabheoc at St. Patrick's altar, and St. Teresa of the Infant Jesus at Our Lady's altar. Monsignor Keown, the former Prior of Lough Derg, who was responsible for the building of this church, made a special journey to Italy with Mr. Cullen, the architect, in order to select personally the marbles used here to such good effect. He spent a happy time in Carrara, which he delights to recall, and visited the famous marble quarries on the Apuan Alps to examine their whole range of products.

The vivid colours of mosaic are used with sparing discrimination to add their effect to this interior : Our Lady and Saint Patrick are depicted in circular mosaic insets at the back of their respective altars. The four evangelists are shown in mosaic panels inset in the Communion rails.

The lighting is unusually cheerful, because the interior walls are white, and there are one hundred and sixty-nine windows, well distributed around the building, providing a lovely contrast of light and shade : the apse is flooded with silvery, lake-reflecting light captured from on high, but the naves are full of luminous shadows, lit only from the stained glass in their windows.

The Stations of the Cross are original, for they are depicted in stained glass windows executed by the late Harry Clarke. Each window shows one of the Twelve Apostles (Judas being of course replaced by Matthias). Saint Paul is added to the Twelve, and Our Blessed Lady is also brought into the scheme to complete the number fourteen. The Apostles are ranged in that order given in the tenth chapter of Saint Matthew's Gospel. Each of these fourteen, the greatest figures in Christian history, holds a Station on an inset plaque of lighter glass, more delicately coloured, so that it stands out in relief. Thus it is the Station of the Cross which holds the attention, while the full-sized figure in the window seems to hover attentively in the back-ground.

Harry Clarke, before he died, was considered the greatest stained glass artist in the world. As the lake and its surroundings are an almost unvarying mono-chrome of brown or grey, the wealth of colour in

these windows is a particular joy. They seem to have
captured all the deepest and loveliest hues : the purple
and ruby of marine pools ; the flaming scarlet and emerald
of Chinese pheasants and macaws ; the glowing rose
and the blues of tropical butterflies, the brilliance of
gladioli and of certain kinds of semi-precious stones.

Accustomed to mass-produced statuary and decoration
—conventional, dead stuff imported from tenth-rate
Continental factories—some pilgrims may find these
windows almost startling, for here is art that is alive.
St. John, for instance, (the Fifth Station), is endowed
by the artist with amazing youthfulness : he has the
exalted expression of a mystic, but he is scarcely out
of his teens. Again, Our Lady, in the Fourteenth
Station, has the face of a mere girl, though it is full of
sorrow and of a kind of stilled devoutness. Each
Apostle is shown with the symbol by which he is known
in Christian art, and the colouring of each window is
also emblematic. All are dressed in gorgeous robes,
richly embroidered and lavishly fringed.

The particular pleasure experienced in this church,
however, does not derive from its adornment, but from
something less tangible and more difficult to describe.
While recognising and saluting the many beautiful
features of that interior : the warmth and glow of the
stained glass (almost like precious jewel caskets) ; the
delicately-coloured marbles, the altars, the pulpit with
its alabaster panels, the exquisitely designed candelabra
(great groups of electric lights suspended from the domed
roof like clusters of gigantic berries), and all the other
lovely accessories so carefully selected and perfectly
placed with a view to harmony—it is not these, but
the balanced and airy spaciousness of this interior that
so particularly exalts the mind. One has the impression
of a vertical column of space springing from the parquet
floor of the church and rising to the roof. It may well
be asked if this illusion of a centrally placed space-
shaft occurs in all buildings capped with domes and
cupolas ? I do not think so. I believe that the balance

of structural masses in St. Patrick's Basilica is unique. The surrounding parts are in comparative gloom, and the glooms seem to press in upon the centre, so that the light forms a kind of Jacob's ladder between floor and dome.

The former St. Patrick's church used to hold about three hundred people but at the cost of much crowding and discomfort. When, as frequently happened early in the twentieth century, one thousand pilgrims found themselves on the island together, only the fortunate three hundred made the night vigil under cover. Assuming that some hundreds would have already made the vigil and would be in bed, several hundred were compelled to make the vigil outside the church, exposed to varying weather conditions. Faced with the absolute necessity of building a new church, the pilgrimage authorities had the courage to build big. The new St. Patrick's has seating accommodation for nineteen hundred people : one thousand on the ground floor and three hundred in each of the three galleries. A remarkable feature is that everybody in the church can see the priest when he is celebrating Mass (except of course those people immediately behind the pulpit). Even if this country were to have its population of pre-Famine days restored, and if it witnessed some transforming, terrific resurgence of faith, and the extraordinary scenes of the 1846 pilgrimage season were repeated, when thirteen hundred pilgrims arrived on the island in a single day, this church could now receive them all without discomfort. If the national pilgrimage of Ireland became in fact what it is in name, the new church could never fail to fulfil its purpose as " a home, roof and gathering-place " for the people (as Belloc said of St. Peter's in Rome).

The Basilica of St. Patrick at Lough Derg is a very special triumph. I do not so much mean that, standing there in its quiet strength and majesty, it is a necessary vindication of the Catholic cause, the final word in the painful struggle that was waged for dominion over this rock in a lake, ground that has no value except the

supreme value of being holy ground. This church represents too another kind of victory. Everywhere else in
the Christian world to-day one visits old artistic monuments of religion, built to express faith and piety, from
which in nearly every case the spirit has now fled. Such
monuments are preserved and great efforts are made to
revitalise them simply in order to call back to life the
magnificent spirit that once inspired them. The exact
opposite has happened in St. Patrick's, where the living
and compelling vitality of an ancient devotion has
imperiously called into life this modern monument of
religious art.

The story of the building of this church makes curious
reading. There was not room for it of course on the
circumscribed ground of the island, already so largely
built over. The greater part of the new church rests on
pillars of reinforced concrete bedded in the rocky floor
of the lake. There was a special contractor for the foundations and three months' hard work were put in at them
in 1925. Then a storm of unusual fury and duration
in one night swept the whole work into the lake. All that
could be seen of it the following morning were a few
planks floating far away near the eastern shore. Those
scattered spars were collected again and the work
recommenced. The church was completed, but not yet
consecrated, when it was discovered that the lake water
has the peculiar property of eroding cement, and therefore the supporting pillars were likely to crumble and
endanger the whole structure. After considerable analysis
and testing, chiefly in laboratories of Cork University
by a specialist in the matter, a special substance was
made up that is actually nourished by the peculiar
properties of the lake water. A wooden frame had then
to be made to go around each of the one hundred and
twenty-three pillars on which the church rests, and each
pillar was re-coated with the special cement, so that now
the pillars acquire greater strength with the passage of
time. But this work of re-conditioning was far more
difficult than the original building : the men had to

work from boats of course, and crouched under the roof of the pillars. The friction tore the coats off their backs ; in fact they could not be kept in coats. Even so, they could only work thus painfully when the lake was calm.

St. Patrick's Church was consecrated on the 17th May 1931 and given the title and dignity of a Minor Basilica. It is the only church in Ireland that is so privileged. This dignity is not conferred without some very special reasons : the church in question must be able to claim either great antiquity, or historical associations of an unusual kind ; it must be a church of large dimensions, having dignity and splendour ; its architectural design usually includes porches. The incumbent of a basilica has the right to use the Papal Arms over the church door and in his official communications ; he may walk under a canopy in the manner of a bishop, preceded by a bell ; for choral dress, he may use the *cappa magna* with ermine in front, or a cotta over the rochet.

An explanation of the term " Minor Basilica " may be desirable. There are only six Major (or Patriarchal) Basilicas in the Christian world. Four of these are in Rome under the particular protection of the Pope : the Lateran, the Vatican, the Ostian and the Liberian Basilicas ; the other two are Franciscan : that of St. Francis in Assisi and that of St. Mary of the Angels (known as the *Porziuncola*). All other Basilicas in the Christian world are " Minor " in rank to the above six great churches.

On the Sunday following the consecration of the new church, that is, the 17th May, special thanksgiving ceremonies were held on the island, Cardinal MacRory presiding in the presence of His Excellency, the Most Rev. Paschal Robinson, the Papal Nuncio. There were also present the Bishops of Clogher, Dromore, Kilmore, Derry, Raphoe, Ardagh, and Down and Connor, and many clergy. Pontifical High Mass was celebrated, and the Bishop of Clogher preached a sermon which was really a full historical review of the Lough Derg pilgrimage. Most of the distinguished laity of the country were present, from the President, Deputies and Senators down to members of the local district councils. The seating accommodation of the new church was completely occupied and the overflow filled the gallery steps and the aisles.

The religious ceremonies were followed by a banquet in the boat-house, at which a large company was entertained. Decorations, chiefly in the Papal colours, made the usually grey setting unrecognisable.

It was a day of unprecedented crowds and of happy, spontaneous rejoicing. Six special excursion trains were run to Pettigo from Belfast, Dublin, Derry, Bundoran, Carrickmacross and Cavan. For Pettigo, painted and decorated from end to end, it was a day of days. The station, where a guard of honour received the Cardinal and the Papal Nuncio, was buried in evergreens and festooned with streamers and scrolls. The mainland waitingrooms and piers, where hundreds arrived by private car, were also decorated, and the boats flew the Papal colours ; even the austere island wore garlands that day.

Pilgrims in the Basilica should not omit a visit to the Acolytes' Sacristy, where two interesting treasures are kept : one is the old wooden altar, poor and shabby, which was removed from the previous church replaced by the new Basilica ; the other is the painting attributed to Murillo, presented to this church by the late Sir John Leslie.

The wooden altar is the crudest and simplest of its kind. Its very poverty and inadequacy will forever make it an object of veneration to pilgrims. It is of common wood, cheaply painted and feebly embellished ; to go to it fresh from the splendour and artistic perfection of the new sanctuary is to make a study in contrasts.

The painting of the Madonna is badly hung, being so high that it is most difficult to get a clear view of its details. Sir John Lavery was of the opinion that it is a genuine product of the Murillo school. Our Lady is represented looking up to heaven, a dull blue cloak thrown over her left shoulder, one end of it clasped in her hands. She has the usual very elongated nose, brown hair, fair complexion and girlish expression of Murillo's many Madonnas. She is clothed in an ample white robe with double sleeves, one close-fitting and the other flowing. Her eyes are raised to Heaven, her face devout. She has not an aureole, but behind her head there is a glow of golden light. There are two winged cherubs' heads in the top right-hand corner and three in the left corner. She stands on the moon, resting on a drift of white cloud and around her feet there is a pretty play of five winged cherubs. One of them, head and shoulders only appearing through the cloud, holds up in his left hand the loose end of Our Lady's cloak, as though feinting to hide in it ; another holds a golden palm in his right hand ; a full-sized cherub sits at Our Lady's feet on the edge of the cloud, holding in his left hand a bunch of lilies and the end of a pink cincture, which is thrown over his left shoulder and passes around his back to be held in his right hand also ; there is a winged cherub fading into the distance in the right foreground ; another full-sized cherub sits at the right of the first one, clasping a musical instrument, which he plays with his right hand.

Monsignor Patrick J. Keown, P.P., V.G., Carrick-macross, Prior of the pilgrimage to Lough Derg for thirty-three years, is chiefly responsible for the Basilica. Monsignor Keown's name has already been several times mentioned in these pages. He it is who made the whole modern history of Lough Derg.

Educated at Saint Macartan's Seminary, Monaghan, he first made the pilgrimage to Lough Derg as a clerical student in 1879. He was ordained in Maynooth in June, 1888 ; the following year, he went back to Lough Derg as an assistant priest, and he continued to go there in that capacity every year for twenty years, with two exceptions when health reasons prevented him. His first appointment after ordination was a teaching post in St. Macartan's College. Here his health broke down ; he was threatened with tuberculosis and, with a view to saving his life, he was sent on the mission, as curate to Kilskeery, County Tyrone, where he spent four years. Here his health improved again so remarkably that he was sent back to St. Macartan's College in 1894, and remained there six years, teaching all subjects. He was appointed Administrator in Monaghan in 1900 and continued to act in this capacity for seven years. In 1907 he was made Parish Priest of Aughnamullen West, where he remained two years. Then he was promoted to the parish of Enniskillen, made Archdeacon, and created Prior of Lough Derg, having now had twenty years' intimate familiarity with the pilgrimage. He was promoted to the parish of Carrickmacross in 1919 and made Dean. He now holds the additional titles of Vicar General and Domestic Prelate to His Holiness.

Monsignor Keown held the office of Prior of Lough Derg from 1909 to 1941, and during those thirty-three years he did not miss a single pilgrimage. His term of office was the longest in history. Failing health and advanced years forced him to relinquish it. His total connection with the island covers a period of sixty-four years, which amounts to an average lifetime. Although carrying out for much of the same period the onerous duties of Parish Priest of the large, thriving town of Carrickmacross, of Dean of the diocese and Vicar General, the real work of his life was devoted to St. Patrick's Purgatory.

The year following his appointment as Prior, he set to work to remedy the lack of accommodation. The building of the present women's hospice was begun in 1910, providing sleeping quarters for three hundred. The joy in the possession of this new building was marred, as we have seen by a typhoid fever outbreak. The Prior had a source of pure water tapped two miles away and a new waterworks provided for the island in 1914. Then the Leslie litigation brought a serious threat of a very different kind to the pilgrimage. The Prior guided this litigation to a successful settlement in 1917, resulting in the purchase of the ferry from the landlord for £2,000. A steady succession of improvements were made as a result of the freedom allowed by this settlement. A good house for the caretaker, new waiting-rooms, piers, and a motor garage providing accommodation for thirty-three cars were rapidly provided on the mainland. A new electric power station was set up on the island, also a landing-stage, and a kiosk to serve as post-office and bookshop. The men's hospice was substantially enlarged. Then came the crowning achievement of the Basilica in 1925. It would be invidious to tell the tale of that labour in terms of money, but the sums of money involved in this case are really formidable : £2,000 for the mere freedom of the ferry ; £116,000 for engineering and building schemes ; £80,000 for the new church.

When Monsignor Keown made his first pilgrimage to Lough Derg as a clerical student in 1879, he received some special inner light on the devotion and to that enlightenment he kept faith. The story of any great fidelity is a great story. He initiated a new and honourable phase in the history of this island. Its visible transformation with new buildings is, however, only a symbol of what actually took place. Monsignor Keown found this ancient rite a primitive affair, almost furtive, with needless hardships of every kind superimposed on the voluntary penance, its high significance endangered by the abuses with which it was overlaid. Pilgrims of that day had to be prepared for rough usage which the timid, the sensitive, or the gently-nurtured could not face as a rule, so that countless numbers were excluded from the devotion by the prevailing conditions. He saw to it that pilgrims should no longer risk incurring virulent disease on the island, or that vermin, dirt, exposure to the elements, vulgarity, or hopeless overcrowding should not add to their discouragement. He lifted up the pilgrimage out of all such defects and set it free. Figures are revealing in this case ; on his first pilgrimage in 1879 1,765 made the pilgrimage ; the yearly number of pilgrims has now steadied to an average of fifteen thousand.

He found pilgrims being mulcted by the railway companies, bullied by car-drivers, overcharged by boat-men, harassed and persecuted by every kind of un-scrupulous profit-maker who battened on their piety. Quietly and persistently, he strove with all these difficul-ties until finally he restored order where disorder had so grievously intruded. Known for forty or fifty years to countless thousands of pilgrims as a stern discip-linarian (if not as a kind of bogey to the incurably frivolous), he functioned in reality as the arch-protector of pilgrims, the defender of quiet souls. On their behalf he quelled abuses with unending vigilance.

A man of average build, with a deceptively mild manner and a tranquil eye, the Dean is a born combatant. When something has to be done, he carries it to its conclusion with a will of iron. He not only eliminated external aggression, but he watched too with a vigilant eye lest abuses should arise among the pilgrims themselves. Among the many thousands who annually frequent the place, there are the inevitable few who go there with the wrong motives : either through curiosity, or in a barely suppressed spirit of tourism, or because they have some false spiritual slant, which is immediately revealed in the searchlight of this penetrating test. In a word, they are prepared to do anything except concentrate on penance. The pilgrimage seems to them hard beyond endurance and they try to escape from it. The obvious way is to make a parade of physical inability. It was Monsignor Keown who built up the great modern tradition, so absolutely sound, that there is simply no escape on the island from its penitential rigours. The rule is inflexible. One is not supposed to go there unless in average health and, having arrived, one must either conform with the pilgrimage ruling, or leave the island. If rest and food seem indispensable, the pilgrim must go back to the mainland for them. If sickness develops, he must likewise return to the mainland for proper care. No pilgrim is allowed to rest on the island, except at the prescribed time, or to eat anything except the prescribed fare. This ruling may seem harsh, but a little reflection will show that it is essential for discipline.

A different type of priest from Monsignor Keown has usually had all the publicity in Ireland : the " soggarth aroon " of song and story, like Canon Sheehan's " New Curate," or Father O'Flynn of the popular song, or the witty Father Healy of Bray. The resurgence of St. Patrick's Purgatory in modern times is due to the work of a priest of very different calibre, or whom much less has been said and written. I mean the solid churchman, of undivided loyalty, who, while remaining unmistakably Gaelic and nothing else, is universalist rather than Irish in outlook, and whose accomplishment is permanent in character. Monsignor Keown gave honourable service to his great namesake, Patrick, during his thirty-three years' administration of a sanctuary which, but for him, might never have survived the many hazards of fortune through which he so faithfully guided it.

XI. MAKING THE PILGRIMAGE

WHETHER the pilgrim to St. Patrick's Purgatory knows it or not, he is a sort of Rip Van Winkle whose experience is reversed : he finds himself catapulted back from the twentieth century into the fifth. If he goes there for the first time, he is on a voyage of discovery in which he will gain experimental knowledge of the past, not merely in his mind but in his very body. The Patrician age endures on the island and fifteen hundred years are almost as though they had never been. Unrivalled peace and isolation give him complete freedom to savour this experience.

He will embark on a mountain-locked lake that is just as secluded to-day as when Saint Patrick was attracted to its solitude. The physical features of the landscape have remained practically unaltered through the centuries. Its lonely aspect is the same as in the fifth century ; the eye may still rest on all that Patrick saw : in the west, Croagh-Breac (the Speckled Stack) ; in the east, Kinnagoe ; behind the one the same solemn sunsets still gild the sky, above the other appear the same fresh dawns.

It is a three-day pilgrimage and a minimum period of residence on the island is prescribed : from three o'clock on the afternoon of the first day to half-past eleven on the morning of the third day. The pilgrim is obliged to fast on each of the three days. When he arrives on the island, his first duty is to remove his shoes. He must go barefoot until he is about to leave the island again. Thus he finds himself at once in the grip of a rigid discipline, extremely uncomfortable. He will probably not like it. He is not meant to like it.

When he reaches the island he usually has not broken his fast since the night before, that being the traditional way to perform the pilgrimage. The practice then is to make at least one Station before taking food. A Station commences with a visit to the Blessed Sacrament in the Basilica. The pilgrim then walks to St. Patrick's Cross, a poor but cherished relic made of rude iron and set on a very ancient stone column. It stands a few yards south of the church entrance. Kneeling before this, he recites one *Pater*, one *Ave* and the Creed.

The shaft on which this iron cross is set is precious, for it was salvaged from the lake. It once formed part of an ancient cross that was broken up and flung into the water, probably at the destruction of 1632. The spiral tracery incised on this column and the three parallel bands forming the capital indicate probable ninth-century origin.

The pilgrim then proceeds to St. Brigid's Cross, which is cut in a block of stone, inset in the left-hand exterior wall of the Basilica. This cross is one of Roman type, deeply incised and believed to date from the twelfth century. The slab on which it is cut was taken from the wall of the old St. Patrick's church, demolished to make room for the present Basilica. Kneeling before this cross, three *Paters*, three *Aves* and the Creed are said. The pilgrim then rises, faces the lake with outstretched arms, his back to the cross, and three times repeats aloud the ancient formula renouncing the World, the Flesh and the Devil. This repetition of the baptismal vow is a reaching back again towards baptismal innocence and is the usual ritual of retreats. But here in the special circumstances it takes on an entirely new meaning. Recited in the open, while facing the airy spaciousness of mountain, sky and water, the pilgrim has the impression of having reached some complete solitude, despite the fact that there is probably a queue of people awaiting their turn beside him.

He must then walk around the Basilica four times, repeating as he walks, seven decades of the Rosary and one Creed. The number of circuits around the old church used to be seven. But the area of the new church being at least three times that of the older one, the

number of circuits is accordingly reduced to fit more
nearly the duration of the prescribed prayers. This is
usually the most pleasant part of the Station, because
most of the circuit is a concrete path, built over the water
at the back of the church.   One has the impression of
walking on the deck of some gigantic ship.

The pilgrim must now proceed to the craggy knoll
in the middle of the island, the real holy ground, venerated
for immemorial ages. Spread out on this slope are the
remains of six beehive cells, or oratories, mere rude
rings of boulders and rough stones, embedded up-end
in the soil.   These are traditionally believed to be the
remains of the cells at one time inhabited by monks
of the Celtic dispensation, who guarded the sanctuary.
They are dedicated to Saints Brigid, Brendan, Catherine,
Columba, Molaise and Dabheoc.   The dedications are
now merely complimentary and it is not claimed that
any of the saints ever used the original cells, with the
possible exception of Dabheoc.   These were the first
saints to be honoured in Ireland and, apart from their
present function, they are an interesting group : Brigid,
the strong-minded agricultural saint, almost contemporary with Patrick, outstanding among the women
converts whom the Apostle found so surprising in their
immediate comprehension of conventual life and their
enthusiasm for it.   Brendan, the indefatigable traveller,
who Christianized uncharted regions of the world ;
Catherine : who was she ? The only one of the group
who might have been really foreign.   There are six
saints of the name : Catherine of Alexandria, Catherine
of Bologna, Catherine of Genoa, Catherine de' Ricci,
Catherine of Siena, Catherine of Sweden.   I think it
likely that this saint of the penal bed is the Franciscan
Saint Catherine of Bologna, whose incorrupt body is
preserved in the Chapel of the Poor Clares in Bologna.
Possibly the Franciscans, who gave St. Mary's Church
its title, brought also with them to the island their
devotion to this Italian mystic.   She had a certain
affinity, too, with Saint Brigid, inasmuch as she was a

great abbess and the founder of convents, and a woman of advanced culture. She wrote a treatise on the spiritual life and there is among the treasures in Oxford a manuscript which she illuminated and which was once the prized possession of Pope Pius IX. It is hardly necessary to speak of Columcille, Abbot of Iona, the prince-missionary of the fiery enthusiasms and immense achievement, who is still the boast of his own people. Molaise, the anchorite of Devenish and one-time ruler of the Clogher diocese, is a peculiarly local saint, as is also Dabheoc, first Abbot of Lough Derg.

In the centre of each rude circle stands a modern bronze crucifix, numbered in its order and named, so that following the exercise presents no difficulty to the beginner. At each of those oratories, or " Beds " as they are called on the island, the devotions are the same : three *Paters*, three *Aveas*, the Creed, repeated four successive times in this wise : while making three circuits of the outside ; while kneeling at the entrance ; while making three circuits of the inside ; and while kneeling at the crucifix in the centre.

The stone circles are small. When this sanctuary was demolished in the seventeenth century the despoilers left only the rude foundation stones protruding from the soil. Over these the pilgrims walk to-day : they are stones not merely sharp, but frequently so steeply inclined on the slope that it is difficult to get a footing on them. When hundreds are making the exercises at the same time, fatigue is trebled in the cramped space. The pilgrims have to kneel as best they can on the jagged rocks ; some of them (aged and excusable) rise by leaning heavily on the shoulders of others, who are still kneeling. To understand the possible misery of it, think of rainy conditions, frequent on the island, when the stones become doubly slippery and the whole slope acquires a slithery and greasy surface.

To do the necessary walking around those Beds, especially the first and second circles, which are very sharply inclined, is in itself almost a physical feat. To do it, as it is done in most cases, after a long railway journey and while fasting, and at the same time to concentrate on the prayers, is a severe test. At first sight, it seems preposterous : the soul rebels violently and has to be dragged along every step of the way, like a spancelled donkey, ceaselessly protesting : not *twelve* Our Fathers and Hail Marys at *every* circle, not all those prayers again here surely ? How is one to pray under such conditions ? Who could put up with anything so ruthlessly monotonous ?

The double circle, known as the " large penitential Bed " in the leaflet of instructions, is ground that is particularly sanctified. The two cells are dedicated to Saints Dabheoc and Molaise respectively. According to the earliest extant maps of the island, the other penal cells have always occupied the same position from earliest ages and they have retained the same dedication at least from the seventeenth century. But this double cell suffered a change of dedication. From the map in Carve's *Lyra Hibernica* (A.D. 1666) it is clear that of those two circles joined together, the one nearer to the water was considerably larger than the other and it was dedicated to Saint Patrick, while the attached smaller cell was dedicated to Saints Dabheoc and Molaise together. Moreover, from the instructions issued to pilgrims in the year 1600, or thereabouts, it is to be remarked that the pilgrim did not go into Patrick's Cell at all : he prayed while walking around outside it, and while kneeling at its entrance, but he did not go in, probably through reverence. It is worth remembering, then, that this larger enclosed space, nearer to the water's edge was considered particularly holy ground for many generations.

When he has completed the round of those six " Beds ", the pilgrim goes to the edge of the water, where five *Paters*, five *Aves* and the Creed are said standing, and the same prayers are repeated kneeling. This escape from the " Beds," those terrible and remorseless circles of stone, is a great assuagement. The pilgrim feels as though an iron yoke had been lifted from the back of his neck and he can now straighten up and breathe. Traditionally, those prayers at the water's edge are recited standing and kneeling on a special stone, some distance out in the water, called " leac-na-moan," or the monk's stone of penance, upon which St. Patrick is supposed to have left the imprint of his knees. This stone is further credited with the virtue of healing the bruised feet of pilgrims. In practice, few pilgrims find it, nor is it in the least necessary to do so. The prescribed prayers are simply said at the water's edge. The pilgrim then returns to St. Patrick's Cross, whence he set out, where he says on his knees one *Pater*, one *Ave* and the Creed. Finally he enters the Basilica, where the Station is concluded by saying five *Paters*, five *Aves* and one Creed for the Pope's intentions. A Station takes about an hour and a quarter to say with recollection.

The pilgrim may now break his fast ; the fare provided is a kind of oaten biscuit eaten dry (which would be quite palatable with butter !), or dry bread, which may be toasted. He has a choice of cold, or hot water, doubtfully " flavoured " with salt and pepper, or sweetened ; or tea without milk, which may be sweetened. He goes into the hostel for it and sits on a long bench at an unfurnished table, the cement floor striking coldly to his bare feet.

On his first day, two more Stations are obligatory, so that shortly he will have to return to the penal cells and spend another two and a half hours saying the same prayers again in the same manner as before. A total of nine of these Stations, or Rounds, have to be said while he is on the island. Three Stations each day was the ancient rule, but the nine were re-divided up in modern times, chiefly to make it possible for the pilgrim to leave the island early on the third day and catch his train for a distant destination. The present ruling is : three Stations the first day, four the second day (recited in the church during the night vigil), and two Stations on the third day. The pilgrim's time is further occupied by two services each evening in the church, one at six and the other at nine. Although hard-pressed for time, the pilgrim may take brief intervals of rest at the turf fire in the hostel where he may enjoy a smoke and a chat. At any time of the day he is free to drink water, cold or hot, or sweetened with sugar, or made interesting with the addition of salt and pepper.

His first night on the island is spent keeping vigil in the church, where the four Stations of obligation for the second day are recited aloud, led by a pilgrim priest, or by a senior pilgrim. There are intervals of fifteen minutes between the Stations, during which he is free to leave the church and walk around outside, the better to ward off sleep. The average man usually finds himself being tortured with the desire for sleep about 2 a.m. There is a leaden weight on his eyelids and he moves and prays like a somnambulist. The choice of prayers seems at first sight to make the vigil still harder. There seems never to be any respite from that terrific iteration of *Paters*, *Aves*, Creeds. During this night of vigil he has to say aloud three hundred and ninety-six *Paters*, six hundred and forty-eight *Aves*, and one hundred and twenty-four Creeds.

The mind is stunned at first by what seems to be such heavy and endless repetition. But when the first stage of listless reaction has passed, the monotony of prayer is found to have the same result as that produced by chanting the liturgy in an unvaried tone : the whole mind is liberated to focus on the words, without the distraction of *coloratura*. Thus when the pilgrim arrives at saying the fiftieth Creed he may at last begin to take note of the words, and at the hundredth he may begin to mean what he says. As he works through his Stations the simple and unvarying prayers composing them begin to rise up hugely, as if a loom stretched from earth to heaven on which the web of life is hung. From having no meaning, they burst with sudden luminosity into a thousand meanings. From saying nothing, they say everything. They are encyclopaedias in the total of languages.

These were certainly the prayers of the seven saints who were the guardians of this sanctuary : Patrick, Brigid, Brendan, Catherine, Columcille, Molaise and Dabheoc. The ancients had not the habit of addressing the Lord in inflated or pretentious petition. They were diffident about making up their own prayers, fearing not to pray acceptably. They kept to the divine models : the prayer taught to the apostles by Christ ; the angel's salutation to Mary ; the prayer of the universal Church. The implication at Lough Derg is that there are still no better prayers than these. They say all and nothing need be added.

An old legend in a life of St. Brendan the Navigator relates how three clerical students went off to a desert island, determined to win Heaven for themselves. They devoted all their days to praying in just such a fashion as one prays during the night vigil on this island. They recited the ancient prayers in enormous blocks and in every posture : standing upright, sitting, kneeling, with outstretched arms, with hands joined. They prayed like athletes drilling, repeating the words almost like physical exercises are repeated, shaking the very stars with their fusillades of Paters. The legend recalls the methods of spiritual training devised by the early Irish Christians and gives a clue to the present-day island practice.

This island ritual insists on the elemental needs of the soul. In nothing is its power and universality shown so clearly as in its choice of prayer. The simplest and the most unlettered Christians can take their part in it without the aid of any book. Too often we pray in pompous, distasteful jargon repeated heedlessly out of compilations of prayers put together by someone as inept as ourselves in the matter of prayer. All such aberrations and mannerisms are discouraged on the island, where one has to get down to bed-rock in spiritual matters.

During one of the intervals between Stations the pilgrim will see dawn come up behind Kinnagoe, its light breaking over the grey water. This is a privileged experience in a place dedicated from the beginning to recollection and peace. Many of the pilgrims are talkative in the early watches of the night, but by dawn a hush seems to fall upon even the most irrepressible. The holy calm of the island begins its work of penetration. At six a.m. the spell is broken by a vigorous clanging of a bell, followed by an answering bustle in the hostels as the outgoing pilgrims rise from their night's sleep. Everyone on the island attends Mass at six-thirty.

The day that follows belongs to the pilgrim to use as he wishes. Now is his opportunity to pray, read, write, think, contemplate ! The pilgrimage lays no duties upon him, provided he goes to Confession during the morning and visits the church at noon. There are no Stations of obligation. Only one thing intrudes to trouble this singular day of leisure and that is the overweening desire for sleep. It is a long day. The time appointed for going to bed is half-past nine. The leaden minutes seem to crawl by on sticky feet that make no progress. The hours hang back. Time stands revengefully still. The pilgrim usually finds he can make no masterly use of these hours for the prayer, the reading, writing and contemplation in which he should be engaged. The hours await him and usually he is too stunned by fasting and lack of sleep to do anything with them except live through them in disappointment and frustration. By afternoon, life has resolved itself into a wrestle with sleep. When he kneels to pray in the church his eye-lids droop and close. If he sits for a moment at the turf fire in the dining-room, sleep seizes him with inescapable mastery. He flees from the warmth to sit on one of the benches outside, only to find the figures of the other pilgrims dissolving into haze around him. By evening, he spends his time running from post to pillar, trying to shake off the enemy.

After Stations of the Cross at 9 p.m. the pilgrims are given access to rooms where there are rows of foot-basins, fixed at floor level, with hot and cold running water, and where towels and soap are in readiness.

Here they prepare for bed by taking a foot-bath. The beds are good but even if they were as hard as planks the sleep that follows would surely be unique. Even to remember it is restful. It is that sleep described by Macbeth when he lost it ; a relief that knits again what care has ravelled, a very balm. One drops like a plummet into a soundless abyss of repose, into depths that are cool and sweet, where no whisper penetrates until the urgent notes of the bell swing the sleepers back into wakefulness at six next morning.

Many pilgrims surveying the crowds during the night vigil promise themselves that, on their following night of freedom, they will look down from their cubicle windows at the fascination of the scene, when the people emerge and group themselves in the loggias. The many windows of the lighted Basilica shine like amber panels in the darkness and all around it is the glint and stir of water. It is like the setting of some superb operatic scene. But I never knew a pilgrim to realize this pleasant project. The fresh air that blows across the lake, bringing the Atlantic ozone from Donegal Bay, makes sleep on the second night an imperious and inescapable necessity when added to the fact that the average pilgrim has put in about forty hours without sleep.

The final morning on the island is a crowded one. The boat leaves at eleven-thirty and there are two Stations, or two and a half hours' prayer of obligation, to be said before leaving. No time may be lost. After Mass the pilgrim has to get to business with alacrity. He may then turn his mind once more to mundane things, collect his belongings and put on footwear.

Everyone on the island gathers at the landing-stage to watch the boat's departure, as this is the chief event of each day. The signal for embarkation is given by the ferryman who, following the ancient and picturesque ceremonial, dons a peaked cap and sounds a long warning note on a bugle. There is an answering bustle and scurry among the pilgrims and soon they begin to stream out from the hostels towards the landing-stage. The boat fills and once more the bugle calls, scattering plaintive echoes over the water. The last-comer is packed on board and the oarsmen stand in readiness. The departing pilgrims are relieved that their ordeal is over, but like the bardic poet, Feargal Mac Ward the Younger, some inexplicable affection binds them to this sanctuary and nearly every face is wistful. Sometimes this gentle melancholy is dissipated by the sight of a belated flying figure emerging through the door of one of the hostels waving frantically. Resignedly a boatman flings across the rope again and the boat is steadied while the very last one who was nearly late is helped on board. Finally, the heavy oars are dipped and the cumbersome barque moves slowly away. Pilgrims remaining on the island wave them off. If there are old-timers on board they raise their voices in the traditional farewell hymn to Lough Derg.

Every boat-load of pilgrims contains a cross-section of human society that has a special interest. Sharp contrasts in age are frequent : two men of ninety have been known to make the pilgrimage in recent years, while girls and boys in their very early teens are always among the crowds. The pilgrims also exhibit marked contrasts in type and condition : women whose clothes, though carefully chosen with a view to simplicity, nevertheless bear the stamp of wealth, are side by side with others clearly on the outermost edge of what is known as decent poverty ; extremely sophisticated city people are thrown into the company of very simple country folk and appear to enjoy it ; on this island, men of genius and learning find common ground with those who are totally illiterate. This passing throng provides an extraordinary study : faces of elderly people, full of rustic contentment, serene, unlined, incurious, and youthful faces full of nameless anxieties, on which every kind of premature experience is stamped and etched. There is a unifying factor, moreover, which makes the crowds to be observed on Station Island more interesting than crowds that gather anywhere else in the world : a common spiritual purpose binds them all ; they are all penitents.

Among the pilgrims there will always be found numbers who constitute records in the matter of fidelity. They have come to the island every year for ten, fifteen or twenty years. So far as is known, the palm in this respect was carried off by an old man who had done the pilgrimage fifty-six times : he had first come to the island in the prime of his manhood, at the age of twenty-four, and then he came every year until he died during the winter following his fifty-sixth pilgrimage, being then over eighty years of age. This was a life to which St. Patrick's Purgatory had formed a mystic undercurrent. In the bewildering mutations of life, this man had found something constant that gave him unfailing satisfaction, so he clung to it. How many human relationships, full of promise and consolation, must he not have seen begun and ended during that period ?

Other pilgrims seek to establish a different sort of record by doubling their period of residence on the island. With some secret purpose in mind, they make two pilgrimages, or even three, without a break, in one mighty effort of heroism. In recent years, about twenty perform a six-day fast every year, and a smaller number a nine-day fast. Special permission has to be obtained to remain on the island longer than the prescribed three days, and this assent is not given without some investigation and study of each particular case.

This rite of great antiquity and prestige is universal in its application and appeal. The fact that it is practised by people from every grade of society, and its remarkable continuity, are proof of its power to satisfy the intimate needs of the soul. Its effect is refreshment, so tonic and abiding that even the ill-used and mortified body shares in that mysterious renewal. The greater number invariably return to repeat the experience.

XII. SPIRIT OF THE PILGRIMAGE

THE Island of St. Patrick's Purgatory stands to the mind of this generation as a kind of Hy-Brasil, or Land of the Blessed. It offers a complete relief to modern conditions of living. It gives deliverance from the feverish bustle of a mechanised age. Time here loses its tyranny. Slaves of clock and calendar, who spend all their years " clocking in " not only on their professional and business hours, but even on their very leisure and on their sleep, are here at last emancipated. This release from the clutches of the clock hands gives a man the freedom that is so necessary for a spiritual adventure.

The pilgrim finds himself cloaked in the most complete and reassuring anonymity. His name has been entered in the official register, true, but this is kept private. He puts his belongings in the cubicle allotted to him and henceforth he is known only by the number of that cubicle. He need reveal his name to no-one unless he likes. He need converse with no-one unless by choice. Many pilgrims prefer to spend their three days in silence. Publicity is debarred here : curious visitors, and still less photographers, are never allowed on the island during the pilgrimage season. When the newcomer casts off his footwear it is a symbol that he is shedding at the same time all those externals that make up status and lend importance to the individual : house, family and dependents, atmosphere, daily occupation. If he is a personage in his ordinary life, he here undergoes an immense levelling and becomes just one of the crowd.

The most attractive aspect of the island routine is that it is a complete suspension of normal living. There is no meal served here in the formal sense, and the usual daily routine of bed, dress and toilet is rudely dislocated. Then there are of course no telephones to distract, or wireless programmes to assail the nerves. There is a complete absence of the fuss, clatter and compulsory absorption in petty trifles that make up the confusion of everyday life. All that bustle, so frequently mistaken for achievement, all that hugger-mugger, is left behind on the mainland and the pilgrim steps into a new air.

I have spoken several times in this book of the presence of crowds on the pilgrimage. Lest a wrong impression be created, however, I must add that the island, though restricted in space, seems completely to absorb crowds, as if by magic. No place can be imagined in which one is more free from the usual chafing of human society. This paradox of solitude in the midst of a mob is explained —I think—by the isolating effect of penance. As an example, take one of the concluding passages of a Station, the lakeside prayer : any pilgrim's arrival at this stage may coincide with that of twenty others, but as he looks out across the water to the mountains, while saying the *Our Fathers* and *Hail Marys*, he is as much alone as if he were on the summit of a hilltop, or in the depths of some primeval forest.

The island is the only place in Ireland, and possibly in Christendom, where the ordinary man has a chance to do physical penance, especially fasting. This opportunity is a boon to the human spirit. It still remains true as in the time of Our Lord, that there are certain devils not to be cast out except by prayer and fasting. The island in this respect fills a need that is as old as Christendom.

It was well named " St. Patrick's Purgatory," not only because a vision of Purgatory was part of its legendary origin, nor because the mortifications imposed here are purgatorial in their severity, but because its very existence suggests a confirmation of the doctrine of Purgatory. Large numbers are strongly drawn to it every year, some of them year after year. They all have available the Sacrament of Penance and the ordinary means of making satisfaction for their sins, but they want to add something more. They are moved by some obscure hunger for justice, for restoring a divine balance, for making retribution. Their free presence is an argument that the human soul in its very nature recognizes the need for Purgatory.

Mention has already been made of the old man who made the pilgrimage every year for fifty-six years in succession. As the fruit of his long association with the island, he must have received a rare degree of self-knowledge. Did he recognise how most evils of our lives are due to our own perverse wills, and was he bent on defeating his own will ? It is evident from his unbroken succession of visits that he found on the island something so divinely precious that it became the pivot of his whole life. The place was his lodestar for more than half a century. He may be taken as a type of Everyman who had discovered a discipline that enabled him to deal with the frailties of humanity, and which indeed satisfies universal human needs. I never met him and I think that conversation with him might have been a great gain. But it is possible also that he may have been totally unable to explain either his motives or his unique experience.

At any rate, he must have discovered what ample provision is made on the island for the seven deadly sins. The pilgrim finds himself a mere number on a hostel list. Pride pales before this disregard and, having nothing on which to feed, it soon vanishes. Bare feet must have been one of the very earliest correctives applied to vain-glory ! The island also caters for gluttony and sloth with an ironical completeness, by offering them— nothing ! The man who thinks too much about food gets, at any rate, food for thought ; the epicure is forced to think about something else. As for sloth, it is simply kicked out of a place where an entire night's sleep has to be sacrificed and where one has to remain about thirty-six hours without any rest at all ; a place where eight and a half hours' sleep are only permitted in three days ; and where whole blocks of prayers, lasting for hours on end, are said by obligation either walking, standing, or kneeling, but not sitting.

Among hundreds of strangers deeply absorbed in their own affairs, the man of choleric temperament, whose life is chiefly diversified by explosions of wrath, will not readily find his usual victim. Moreover, the pilgrim may take with him only the barest essentials, not even a rug for protection against the night air. Everyone on the island is therefore poor, for the time being. In a place where the usual parade of possessions is not a feature, neither avarice nor envy can get any security of foothold.

There is no need to go through the doleful category of moral infirmities. All men, indeed, inherit as the legacy of original sin, vicious tendencies, rebellious inclinations, and sinful habits. These evil propensities given free rein soon lead to sin. Only by prayer and fasting can this concupiscence of our fallen nature be checked and cast out. Where else, if not upon the lonely island with its complete negation of all things gratifying to the natural instincts, can the poor pilgrim seek regeneration and live even for a short triduum that better way of life, that great Christian paradox in its most rigorous interpretation " He that shall lose his life shall find it." The Celtic temperament from the foundation of the Church in Ireland was ever attuned to the doctrine of abnegation. The Lough Derg Pilgrimage, translates into concrete terms the Divine remedy for the conquest over self.

The best book for spiritual reading on the island is St. Patrick's *Confession*. It is to be preferred even to the ubiquitous *Imitation of Christ*. It may be bought very cheaply for sixpence, in convenient pamphlet form, not, unfortunately, published by a Catholic firm, but by the Society for the Promotion of Christian Knowledge. This English translation, by Dr. Newport J. D. White, is wholly reliable. The booklet can be read attentively in half-an-hour, so it is reading that would not be a heavy tax on the pilgrim's power of concentration.

It is almost indispensable reading, because the island routine wonderfully explains St. Patrick, just as his autobiography explains the island. Saint Patrick was a Roman citizen who exhibited the best qualities of his race, perfected by grace : he was simple, direct, honest, and possessed of tremendous physical fortitude. In his spiritual autobiography it never occurs to him to justify himself by anything else except the labour he has put into his work and the toils he has endured. He almost boasts that he has made his body a serviceable instrument, able to stand exposure to the elements, extremes of heat and cold, vigil, prolonged solitude, hunger and thirst, long journeys. He was convinced that the apostolate demanded that particular kind of service.

In close imitation of their apostle, the early Irish churchmen were always strongly ascetical in character. During that great exodus of Irish missionaries to the Continent from the sixth to the ninth century their capacity for penance and endurance was such that it excited comment everywhere they went. The Rule of Saint Columbanus of Bobbio exacted from a monk the most complete kind of self-sacrifice that has ever been described : utter obedience, perpetual silence, except for an essential reason ; a strictly vegetarian diet and only one full meal a day. The vigils and prayers said in choir were more prolonged than those laid down in any subsequent Rule.

So many platitudes have been written about that missionary effort, about the Island of Saints and Scholars having lighted the torch in Europe, that the subject has become trite and almost a matter for derision. But even a mountain of platitudes cannot destroy the basis of truth on which it is erected. The point I want to make here is that those missionaries were men who loathed the accepted order of things which they found. They not only passionately believed that they could change the whole face of the world, but actually they

N

did so change it. That regenerating force which they propagated with such fierce and irresistible energy has long since spent itself. The Penitential of Saint Columbanus has long since been superseded by the gentler rule of Saint Benedict. The spirit of asceticism has become attenuated in Christendom, with the Advent fast gone and the Lenten observance so modified and so largely reduced to mere almsgiving; it is still preserved only among certain orders of religious. But here on this island the authentic echo of Patrick's voice can still be heard, diminished it is true by the passage of centuries, but still perfectly audible. The great movement of conversion that he initiated operated strongly for three centuries, almost nine generations, but its effects are eternal. The penitential spirit that was its driving-force still lives on to-day in this remote Donegal island.

If Saint Patrick is worth finding and knowing, the pilgrim to Lough Derg, armed with the *Confession* has the key to that knowledge. The writing is a deeply interesting self-portrait of a man who had conquered himself in a hundred bloodless battles before he set out to add a new realm to the Kingdom of God on earth. The island routine is a complete illustration of his method.

The *Confession* contains this moving prayer :

" Let it not happen to me from my God that I should ever part from his people whom he purchased in the ends of the earth . . . to give me perseverance . . . . that I may bear faithful witness to him, until my passing hence . . . . "

Nowhere has that prayer been so strikingly answered as in the Purgatory, where the personal link has been maintained unbroken for fifteen hundred years. Here the Apostle and his own people, whom he so genuinely loved, are bound together in an eternal kinship. From this island within an island he has never been ousted. This is his impregnable citadel that has never been taken.

FINIS.

NOTES AND DOCUMENTATION

CHAPTER I

p. 3. *The Tripartite Life of St. Patrick*. Edited by Dr. Whitley Stokes, Rolls Series, London, 1887.

The Breviarium of Tirechan is preserved in *Liber Ardmachanus*, The Book of Armagh, edited with Introduction and Appendices by John Gwynn, D.D. Dublin : Hodges Figgis, 1913.

pp. 3, This elucidation was offered by Professor Eoin
4. MacNeill in a letter to Monsignor P. Keown.

p. 5. Archbishop Healy's *Life and Writings of St. Patrick*, p. 299.

p. 6. Adamnan : *Life of St. Columba*. Edited by William Reeves. Dublin, 1857.

p. 7. St. Fiacc's Hymn, in the *Tripartite Life*, edited by Whitley Stokes. Cf. Eoin MacNeill's *St. Patrick*, p. 80.

p. 8. Cf. *Tripartite Life*, Chap. III.

p. 9. ,, *idem*, p. 265.

p. 9. *The Writings of St. Patrick*, translated by Newport J. D. White, London, S.P.C.K., 1932.

CHAPTER II

p. 15. Cf. Professor Eoin MacNeill's *St. Patrick*, p. 55, for an interesting note on missionaries from Wales coming to help St. Patrick.

p. 20. Adamnan.

p. 21. ,, *The Four Masters*, O'Donovan, Dublin, 1851.

p. 21. H. C. Lawlor : *The Monastery of St. Mochaoi of Nendrum*. Belfast, 1925.

Chapter III

p. 27. Stuart's *History of Armagh*, edited by Rev. Ambrose Coleman, O.P.

p. 29. John Colgan's *Trias Thaumaturga*, pp. 273–280. Appendix VI. *De Purgatorio S. Patricii*.

    c.f. *Hermathena*, No. XLIV, " *St. Patrick's Purgatory—a German account*," and *Englische Studien*, Vol. I, pp. 57–121, by L. Toulmin-Smith.

p. 31. Juan Perez de Montalban. *Histoire de la Vie et du Purgatoire de S. Patrice*. 1661.

p. 33. Shane Leslie. *St. Patrick's Purgatory*, 1932. pp. xvii and 6–7.

p. 37. *Le Lettere di S. Caterina da Siena* a cura di Piero Misciattelli. Vol. III, p. 219. Siena, 1913.

Chapter IV

The primal sources of most of the references in this Chapter may be found in Canon O'Connor's *History* and Shane Leslie's compilation.

Chapter V

p. 56. Cf. Shane Leslie, pp. 163–180.

    Aodh de Blacam. *Gaelic Literature Surveyed*.

    Rev. L. McKenna. *Dioghluim Dána* and *Dán Dé*.

    T. F. O'Rahilly. *Irish Poets, Historians and Judges in English*.

    E. Knott. *Irish Syllabic Poetry*.

    The poem by Donnchadh Mór Ó Dálaigh is contained in fourteen manuscripts in the Royal Irish Academy collection, as follows: 23D 13, 23C 27, 23B 35, 23L 6, 24L 6, 23N 35, 24B 26, 23L 34, Fvi 1, Fii 2, 23C 23, 24M 4, 23C 19, and 3B 7. It is worth noting that nine of those MSS. ascribe the poem to Ó Dálaigh, four of them do not give an author and one MS. (23C 23) ascribes it to Aonghus Ó Dálaigh Fionn.

p. 57. Very Rev. Fr. E. C. Ward, Prior of Lough Derg, says : " Judging by the language and style of the versification, it would not be safe to place the poem earlier than the end of the 17th or the beginning of the 18th century."

p. 61. Cf. Miss T. Condon in *Lia Fail*, I, 1–48 (1924). Also Ossianic Society Publications, vol. VI, edited by John O'Daly, 1858.

Chapters VI and VII

Canon O'Connor's *History* and Shane Leslie's compilation contain all the references to primal sources.

Chapter VIII

The full account of this trial has already been published in a booklet, *The Ownership of Station Island, Lough Derg*, by Margaret Gibbons.

Chapter XI

p. 169. The choice lies between Saint Catherine of Alexandria (c. 310) and the Franciscan Saint Catherine of Bologna (1413–1463). There was great popular devotion to Saint Catherine of Alexandria in the fourth and fifth centuries, but later the cult seems to have died out and was not revived. It does not seem possible to ascertain at what date the " Bed " in question received its dedication but hardly, I think, in Celtic times. All things considered, it seems more likely that the saint here honoured is the Franciscan Catherine. In the poem on Lough Derg by Angus Mac Hugh Roe O Higginn (fl. 1590), there is mention of St. Catherine in connection with the penance, so the dedication is at least as old as that.

BIBLIOGRAPHY

(A selected list, arranged alphabetically under names
of Authors, or Editors.)

Alessandro d'Ancona. *I Precursori di Dante.* Firenze, Sansoni, 1874.

Aodh de Blacam. *Gaelic Literature Surveyed.*

François Bouillon. *Histoire de la Vie et du Purgatoire de S. Patrice.* (Rouen, 1701).

C. S. Boswell. *An Irish Precursor of Dante.* Grimm Library. London, 1908.

Sir A. Boswell. *Brief Memorial of the Life and Death of Dr. James Spottiswoode.*

J. B. Bury. *Life of St. Patrick and His Place in History.* London, Macmillan, 1905.

Pedro Calderon de la Barca. *Dramas.* Translated from the Spanish by Denis Florence M'Carthy. Vol. II.

William Carleton. *Father Butler. The Lough Derg Pilgrim.*

Giacomo Certani. *Vita del prodigioso S. Patrizio . . . . Con la veredica storia di L. Ennio.* 1757.

Rev. Ambrose Coleman, O.P. *Stuart's History of Armagh.*

John Colgan. *Trias Thaumaturga. Vita Septima.* Also Appendix VI. *De Purgatorio S. Patricii.*

Miss T. Condon. *Lia Fail.*

Delehaye Father. *Analecta Bollandiana*—tom. XXVII.

Samuel Dillon. Sketches of scenery, history and antiquities in the north-west of Ireland, 1818.

Celso Faleoni. *Teatro delle Glorie, e Purgatorio de' viventi del gran patriarca S. Patricio,* 1657.

Philippe de Felice. *Le Purgatoire de Saint Patrice.* 1906.

H. Gaidoz. *Pilgrimage of the Hungarian nobleman to St. Patrick's Purgatory.* In *Révue Celtique,* II, pp. 482–4, 1872.

Margaret Gibbons. *The Ownership of Station Island, Lough Derg.*

Giraldus Cambrensis. *Historical Works,* with Translations. London : Bell, 1894.

Dom Louis Gougaud. *Christianity in Celtic Lands.* Sheed & Ward, London, 1932.

Rev. John Gwynn, D.D. *Liber Ardmachanus. The Book of Armagh.* Dublin : Hodges Figgis, 1913.

Edward Hayes. *Ballads of Ireland.*

James Hardiman. *Irish Minstrelsy.*

Most Rev. Dr. Healy (Archbishop of Tuam). *Life and Writings of St. Patrick.* Dublin, 1905.

Hermathena, Vol. XL. " Two Early Tours in Ireland." Rev. J. P. Mahaffy, D.D.

Hermathena, Vol. XLIV. " St. Patrick's Purgatory: a German Account." G. Waterhouse.

Archdeacon Hewson's *St. Patrick's Purgatory*, bound in the same volume with John Richardson's account, q.v.

Alfred Jeanroy and A. Vignaux. *Voyage au Purgatoire de St. Patrice.* Toulouse, 1903.

T. A. Jenkins. *Marie de France: L'Espurgatoire Saint Patriz.* 1894.

Jocelin. The Life and Acts of Saint Patrick. Edmund L. Swift. Dublin: 1809.

Bishop Henry Jones. *Saint Patrick's Purgatory.* London: 1647.

James F. Kenney. *The Sources for the Early History of Ireland.* Vol. I. New York. 1929.

Knott, E. *Irish Syllabic Poetry.*

Rev. John Lanigan. *An Ecclesiastical History of Ireland.* Vol. I. Dublin: 1822.

H. C. Lawlor. *The Monastery of St. Mochaoi of Nendrum.* Belfast: 1925.

Shane Leslie. *Lough Derg in Ulster.* 1909.
> *The Story of St. Patrick's Purgatory.* 1917. (This is an American reprint of the earlier work, under a different title.)
> *St. Patrick's Purgatory.* A Record from History and Literature. London: Burns Oates & Washbourne, Ltd., 1932.

H. R. Luard, ed. *Matthew Paris. Chronica Maiora.* Rolls Series. London: 1872–80.

Rev. L. McKenna. *Dán Dé.*

Eoin MacNeill. *St. Patrick, Apostle of Ireland.* London: 1934.
> *Phases of Irish History.* Dublin: Gill, 1919.
> *Celtic Ireland.* Dublin: Lester, 1921.

Rev. C. P. Meehan. *The Rise and Fall of the Irish Franciscan Monasteries.*

Thomas Messinghamus. *Florilegium Insulae Sanctorum.* Paris: 1624.

Migne. *Patrologia Latina*. Vol. 180. 1902.

Piero Misciattelli. *Le Lettere di S. Caterina*, Vol. III. Siena, 1921.

Juan Perez de Montalban. *Histoire de la Vie et du Purgatoire de S. Patrice*. 1661.

Rev. D. Canon O'Connor. *St. Patrick's Purgatory, Lough Derg*. Dublin : 1931.

John O'Donovan. *Annals of The Kingdom of Ireland by the Four Masters*. Vol. IV. 1851.
Donegal Letters, 28th October, 1835.

Sean O'Faolain. *The Great O'Neill*. A Biography of Hugh O'Neill (1550–1616).

Patrick L. O'Madden. *An Irish Church Historian*.

T. F. O'Rahilly. *Irish Poets, Historians and Judges in English Documents*.

Caesar Otway. *Sketches in Ireland*. 1827.

C. Plummer. *Lives of Irish Saints*. Two vols. Oxford : Clarendon Press, 1922.

William Reeves. *Adamnan : Life of St. Columba*. Dublin : 1857.

John Richardson. *The great Folly, Superstition and Idolatry of Pilgrimages in Ireland. Especially of that to St. Patrick's Purgatory*. Dublin : 1727.

Rev. John Ryan. *Irish Monasticism*. Dublin : 1931.

Canon St. John Seymour. *St. Patrick's Purgatory*. Dundalk, 1918.

Rev. J. F. Shearman. *Loca Patriciana*. Dublin : 1879.

Rev. Philip Skelton. *Account of Lough Derg*, Vol. V of *Complete Works*. 1854.

Lucy Toulmin Smith. *St. Patrick's Purgatory and the Knight Sir Owen*. Englische Studien. Vol. I. pp. 57–121.

Whitley Stokes. *The Tripartite Life of Patrick*. (Rolls Series). London : 1887.

Ulster Journal of Archaeology. Special volume on James Spottiswoode, by the Earl of Belmore. Belfast : 1903.

Jacobus de Voragine. *Golden Legend*.

Dr. J. D. Newport White. *St. Patrick : His Life and Writings*. New York : Macmillan, 1920.

Thomas Wright. *St. Patrick's Purgatory*. London, 1844.

Jacobus Yonge. *Le Pélerinage de Laurent de Pasztho au Purgatoire de S. Patrice*. 1908.

INDEX

A

Adamnan, 20, 22, 36.
Aidan, 19.
Alberic, 36.
Alexander VI, Pope, 52, 55.
Allingham, 14.
Anne, Queen, Act of, 84, 108.
Antrim, Lord, 81.
Archdale, Edward, 75.
Ardstraw, 4, 16.
Areskon Archbald, 75.
"Argenta" pilgrimage, 147.
Ariosto, 37, 121.
Armagh, 3, 4, 27, Archdeacon of, 85, Bishop of, 6, Book of, 3.
Ash, 14.
Assaroe, 4.
Aughyarren, 109.
Augustine, Saint, Canons Regular of, 21, 23, 27, 28, 71.
Auxerre, Louis d', 44.
Avil, 19.

B.

Balfour, Lord, 72.
Ballykinlar "pilgrimage," 143.
Ballymacavanny, 18, 110, 135.
Ballyshannon, 4.
Bann, 4.
Bangor, 19.
Barnesmore, Pass of, 4.
Basilica of St. Patrick, 17, 152 et seq., Consecration of, 160 et seq.
Belfast Archaeological Society, 21, 22, Museum, 22.
Benedict XII, Pope, 45.
Bernard, Saint, 20.
Bilberry Island, 14.
Blake, Bishop of Dromore, Diary of, 106.
Bobbio, 20.
Bompton, John, 35.
Blennerhasset, Leonard, 75.
Brendan, Voyage of St. 36, 61, 67, 68, 86.

Brennan's Hotel, 109.
Breviarium of Bishop Tirechan, 3, 4.
Brigid, St., 61, 67, 68, 86 ; Chair of, 16, 18, 19.
Bulkeley, Archbishop, 71.
Bull's Island, 15.

C.

Calderon de la Barca, Pedro, 37, 121.
Campbell, Daniel, 111, 114.
Campion, Edmund, 55.
Canon of Waterford, 48.
Caoranach, 91.
Carleton, William, 88, 91 et seq.
Car-drivers, 148, 149.
Carricknamaddy, Lake, 138.
Carve, Father Thomas (Lyra Hibernica), 102, 171.
Cashel, Psalter of, 68.
Castlederg, 109.
Cataldus, Saint, 20.
Catherine, St., 61, 67, 86.
Catherine, St., of Siena, 37 et seq.
Caxton's Mirror of the World, 48.
Chancellor, Lord, 72, 73.
Charlemagne, 20.
Charles I, 81.
Chiericati, Francesco, 54.
Cillene, 19.
Cistercians, 27.
Clarke, Harry, 156.
Clonard, 19.
Clonfert, 19.
Clonmacnoise, 19.
Coleraine, 4.
Colgan, 16.
Colhoun, Alexander, 97.
Columbanus, 20.
Columcille, 16, 19, 20, 61, 67, 86.
Comedy, Dante's, 35, 36.
Confession, St. Patrick's, 9, 10, 12, 13, 182.
Cooke, Judge, 119.

Cork, Earl of, 72, 73.
Council, Privy, 72, 73.
Crichton, George, 117, 128.
Crissaphan, Georgius, 42, 47.
Croagh Patrick, 7.
Cruise, Bridget, 104.
Crusade, 29.
Cullen, T. J., 153, 156.

D.

Dabheoc Saint, 15, 16, 17, 18,
    19, 21, 22, 23, 26, 61, 67, 68,
    86.
Dane, Mr., 129.
Danes, 21, 23.
Dante, 35, 36, 37, 121.
Dearg-Beg, 14.
Derg-More, 14.
Devorgilla, 42.
Donegal, 1, 12, 109.
Down, Co., 21.
Duffy, Fr. Eugene, 101.
Dundarre, Sir John, 75.
Dunleavy, James, 134.

E.

Eagles' Rock, 14.
Eymstadt, Monk of, 50 et seq.,
    100.

F.

Fiacc, St., 7, 11.
Finn Loch, 14.
Flight of the Earls, 70.
Flood John, 118, 120, 123.
Four Masters, 21, 56.
France, 20.
Franciscans, 70, 97, 98.
Fridolin, St., 19.
Froissart, 44.
Fursey, Vision of, 36.

G.

Gaffney, Rev. John, 101.
Gall, St., 19.

Gavelands, 14.
Georgius, Knight of Hungary, 97.
Germany, 20.
Gilbert, Father, 29, 30, 31.
Giraldus Cambrensis, 16.
Grosjean, Fr., S.J., 66.
Gwynn, Dr. John, 4.

H.

Hardy, 88.
Healy, Dr. John, 5.
Henry, D. S., 130.
Henrietta Maria, Queen, 81, 82,
    87.
Hewson, Archdeacon, 87, 88, 89.
Higden, Ralph, 35.
Holinshed's Chronicles, 55.
Holy Land, 29.

I.

Indulgences, 140.
Inglis, 88, 106.
Inishgoosk Island, 15.
Iona, 19, 20.
Island, Bull's, 15.
   ,,   Friars', 14, 15, 105.
   ,,   Goat, 14.
   ,,   Kelly's, 14.
   ,,   Mahee, 21, 22.
   ,,   Saints', 2, 8, 14, 19, 20
           et seq., 62, 65, 71, 74,
           84, 89, 99, 100, 105,
           109, 112, 127.
   ,,   Station, 2, 8, 9, 11, 14,
           19, 27, 77, 98, 99, 100,
           105, 108, 112, 114, 115,
           121, 127, 135, 138.
   ,,   Stormy, 14.
   ,,   Trough, 14.
Italy, 20.
Ives, St., 46.

J.

James the Less, 12.
John, Saint, 17.
John, Saint, of Bridlington, 45.
John, Don, Carthusian, 38.
John, King of Arragon, 45.
Jones, Henry, 88, 89.

K.

Keating, 42.
Kenney, 12.
Keown, Monsignor P. J., 117, 118, 119 *et seq.*, 124, 126, 127, 128, 134, 136, 156, 162 *et seq.*
Kevin, St., 16.
Killeter, 109.

L.

Lanigan, 88, 93.
Lannoy, Guillebert de, 54.
Lardner, Mr., 119, 120, 121, 124.
Lavery, Sir John, 137.
Ledwich Edward, 102.
Leslie, Charles, 119.
Leslie, Bishop John, 113, 126, 131.
Leslie, Sir John, 19, 109, 115, 117 to 125, 127 to 130, 132, 133, 134, 136, 161.
Leslie, Sir Shane, 137, 150.
Lindisfarne, 19.
Lisle, 44.
Loca Patriciana, 16.
Loch Derc, 14.
Loch Gerg, 14.
Logue, Cardinal, 139, 140.
Lords Justices, 72, 75.
Lough Derg, 1, 13, 16, 17, 27, 28, 29.
Lough Erne, 16, 21, 110.
Lover, Samuel, 104.
Ludlow, 29, 30.
Luxeuil, 20.
Lynch Archbishop, 116.

M.

MacCarthy, Denis Florence, 37, 121.
MacCullen, Art, 90.
McGee, Thomas D'Arcy, 50, 121.
M'Kegan, John, 101.
M'Kenna, Bishop, 134.
M'Kenna, Canon, 103, 115.
MacMahon, Bishop Hugh, 94, 97.
MacMurrough, Diarmuid, 42.
M'Nally, Dr., 114.

MacNeill, Eoin, 14.
MacWard, Feargal, the Younger, 59.
Madeleine, 49.
Magrath, Donough, 62, 63, 64, 65, 112, 126.
Magrath, Master James, 73, 74, 75, 76, 77, 81, 113.
Magrath, Margaret, 128.
Magrath, Mark, 90.
Magrath, Miler, 63 *et seq.*, 113.
Maguire, Mary, 104.
Malachy, Saint, 27.
Mannini, Antonio, 47, 99.
Marie de France, 35.
Mary, Blessed Virgin—of the Angels, 110.
Maxwell, James, 90.
Messingham, 101.
Mochaoi Saint, 22.
Molaise, Saint, 61, 67, 68, 86.
Montalvan, Juan Perez de, 31, 33.
Mulchonry, Torny, 101.
Muldoon, Mary, 118, 120, 126.
Muldoon, Robert, 114, 118, 124, 126, 128.
Muldoon, Thomas, 116, 117, 120, 121, 126, 128, 130.
Mulligan, William, 114.
Murillo, 136, 137, 161.
Murray, Dr., 93.

N.

Nendrum, 21, 22.
Newtown Stewart, 4.

O.

O'Carolan, Florence, 30.
O'Carolan, Turlough, 104.
O'Clery, Michael, 66, 68.
O'Connor, Canon, 92, 93, 102.
O'Dalaigh, Donnchadh Mor, 56.
O'Doherty, Fr. Anthony, 110.
O'Donovan, John, 14, 24.
O'Hara, 57.
O'Higginn, Angus MacHugh Roe, 60, 68.
O'Higginn, Feargal the Younger, 58.

O'Higginn, Tadhg Dall, 57.
O'Maolchonaire, Tuileagna Mac Torna, 58.
O'Neill, the Great, 83.
O'Neill, Niall Og, 45.
O'Neill, Turlough Lynagh, 59.
O'Reilly, Primate Hugh, 70, 71.
O'Rourke, Sir Brian, 65.
O'Rourke, Tiernan, 42.
Otway, Caesar, 88, 92, 93, 94.
Owen Knight, 29 *et seq.*, 37, 38, 41, 42, 56, 99.

P.

Paris, Matthew, 35.
Patmos, 17.
Patrick, St., 3, 67, 86.
Perelhos, Raymond de, 44, 53.
Pettigo, 1, 5, 17, 109, 144.
Philip Boy, 14.
Portcreevy, 16.
Purgatory, St. Patrick's, 2, 7, 9, 27.
Pyrrhus, Ludovicus, 90.

R.

Rathold, Lawrence, 46.
Ratisbon, 20.
Raymond, Count, 49.
Reid, Mr., 119, 120, 123, 128, 134.
Rhine country, 19.
Riaz, Don Diego, 50.
Richardson, 88, 89.
Rinnucinni, 83.
Riordan, Mr. James, 128, 129.
Royal Irish Academy, 68.
Russell, Lord John, 92.

S.

Saltrey, Brother H. of, 30, 31, 33, 35, 36, 37, 47, 56.
Scott, Professor W. A., 152, 153.
Seadavog, 18.
Sergeant-at-Arms, 74.
Skelton, B. M., 117.
Skelton, Philip, 88, 91.
Slemish, Mount, 10.

Smith, Canon, 111, 128.
Smith, Fr. James, 93.
Spottiswoode, 77 *et seq.*, 88, 89, 113, 126.
Staunton, William, 45.
Stephen, King, 29.
Strangford Lough, 21.
Stuart, Sir William, 72, 73, 74.
" Surrender and Re-grant," 62.
Switzerland, 19, 20.

T.

Tara, 16.
Tarleton, Edward, 75.
Templecarne, 5, 7, 8, 13, 15, 25, 61, 62, 85, 91, 105, 110.
Termon-Dabheoc, 15, 61.
Termon-Magrath, 62, 63, 74, 81, 112, 113.
Theodosia, 32.
Tirechan, 3, 4, 5.
Tirhugh, 4, 5, 85.
Tripartite Life, 3, 4.
" The Trouble," 144, 145, 146.
Tundale, Vision of, 36.
Turkill, Vision of, 30.
Twelve Apostles of Ireland, 16.
Tyrone, 4.

U.

Ugolino, 49, 50.
Ulster, Annals of, 53, 54.
Ulster, Excursions in, 106.

V.

Valencia, 32.
Voragine, Jacobus de, 35.

W.

Walsh, Sir Nicholas, 58.
Ware, Sir James, 102.
Wendover, Roger, 35.
Wentworth, Lord, 81, 82, 83, 87.
White, Dr. Newport J. D., 182.
Wright, 88.
Wylie, Mr. W. E., 136.